B1/B2

English for
Today's Workplace

SHORT COURSE SERIES

Angela Lloyd

Dieses Buch als E-Book nutzen:
Use this book as an e-book:
mein.cornelsen.de

zexe-cg-m9gj

Cornelsen

English for Today's Workplace

B1/B2

SHORT COURSE SERIES

Autorin: Angela Lloyd
Beratende Mitwirkung: Marion Karg
Redaktion: Robert Baltzer
Umschlaggestaltung: Studio SYBERG, Berlin

Umschlagfoto: Shutterstock.com/G-Stock Studio
Layoutkonzept: Studio SYBERG, Berlin
Layout und technische Umsetzung:
PER MEDIEN & MARKETING GmbH, Braunschweig

Bildquellen:
S. 3/1: Shutterstock.com/fizkes; **S. 3/2:** Shutterstock.com/Song_about_summer; **S. 3/3:** Shutterstock.com/fizkes; **S. 3/4:** Shutterstock.com/ImYanis; **S. 3/5:** Shutterstock.com/Ground Picture; **S. 3/6:** Shutterstock.com/metamorworks; **S. 6/m.:** Shutterstock.com/Song_about_summer; **S. 6/o.:** Shutterstock.com/fizkes; **S. 6/u.:** Shutterstock.com/fizkes; **S. 7/m.:** Shutterstock.com/Ground Picture; **S. 7/o.:** Shutterstock.com/ImYanis; **S. 7/u.:** Shutterstock.com/metamorworks; **S. 8:** Shutterstock.com/fizkes; **S. 9/A:** Shutterstock.com/Kateryna Onyshchuk; **S. 9/B:** Shutterstock.com/New Africa; **S. 9/C:** Shutterstock.com/fizkes; **S. 9/D:** stock.adobe.com/Liubomir; **S. 10:** Shutterstock.com/sirtravelalot; **S. 12:** Shutterstock.com/Catarina Belova; **S. 14/l.:** Shutterstock.com/Cris Canton; **S. 14/m.:** Shutterstock.com/Phovoir; **S. 14/r.:** Shutterstock.com/Krakenimages.com; **S. 15/A:** Shutterstock.com/Drazen Zigic; **S. 15/B:** Shutterstock.com/paulzhuk; **S. 15/C:** Shutterstock.com/Mangostar; **S. 18/m.:** Shutterstock.com/LightField Studios; **S. 18/o.:** Shutterstock.com/Song_about_summer; **S. 20:** Shutterstock.com/Nadia Snopek; **S. 21:** Shutterstock.com/GBJSTOCK; **S. 23:** Shutterstock.com/fizkes; **S. 26/l.:** Shutterstock.com/fizkes; **S. 26/r.:** Shutterstock.com/voronaman; **S. 27:** Shutterstock.com/Ground Picture; **S. 28:** Shutterstock.com/fizkes; **S. 30:** Shutterstock.com/Drazen Zigic; **S. 31:** Shutterstock.com/Krakenimages.com; **S. 32:** stock.adobe.com/streptococcus; **S. 36:** stock.adobe.com/Kadmy; **S. 37:** Shutterstock.com/Stokkete; **S. 38:** Shutterstock.com/ImYanis; **S. 40/m.r.:** Shutterstock.com/Gorodenkoff; **S. 40/u.l.:** Shutterstock.com/Below the Sky; **S. 40/u.m.:** Shutterstock.com/Aiempp147; **S. 40/u.r.:** Shutterstock.com/ImageFlow; **S. 41/a:** Shutterstock.com/metamorworks; **S. 41/b:** Shutterstock.com/SofikoS; **S. 41/c:** Shutterstock.com/Monkey Business Images; **S. 41/d:** Shutterstock.com/SeventyFour; **S. 41/e:** Shutterstock.com/Gorodenkoff; **S. 41/f:** Shutterstock.com/Monkey Business Images; **S. 44:** stock.adobe.com/Tricky Shark; **S. 48:** Shutterstock.com/Ground Picture; **S. 49:** Shutterstock.com/Monkey Business Images; **S. 50:** Shutterstock.com/Gorgev; **S. 52:** Shutterstock.com/Hryshchyshen Serhii; **S. 53:** Shutterstock.com/ Andrey_Popov; **S. 55:** stock.adobe.com/Studio Romantic; **S. 57:** Shutterstock.com/PeopleImages.com - Yuri A; **S. 58:** Shutterstock.com/metamorworks; **S. 61:** Shutterstock.com/SeventyFour; **S. 63:** Shutterstock.com/Melinda Nagy; **S. 64:** Shutterstock.com/Kzenon; **S. 65:** Shutterstock.com/Monkey Business Images; **S. 67:** Shutterstock.com/Arsenii Palivoda.

www.cornelsen.de

1. Auflage, 1. Druck 2024

Alle Drucke dieser Auflage sind inhaltlich unverändert und können im Unterricht nebeneinander verwendet werden.

© 2024 Cornelsen Verlag GmbH, Mecklenburgische Str. 53, 14197 Berlin

Das Werk und seine Teile sind urheberrechtlich geschützt. Jede Nutzung in anderen als den gesetzlich zugelassenen Fällen bedarf der vorherigen schriftlichen Einwilligung des Verlages. Hinweis zu §§ 60 a, 60 b UrhG: Weder das Werk noch seine Teile dürfen ohne eine solche Einwilligung an Schulen oder in Unterrichts- und Lehrmedien (§ 60 b Abs. 3 UrhG) vervielfältigt, insbesondere kopiert oder eingescannt, verbreitet oder in ein Netzwerk eingestellt oder sonst öffentlich zugänglich gemacht oder wiedergegeben werden. Dies gilt auch für Intranets von Schulen und anderen Bildungseinrichtungen.

Druck: Mohn Media Mohndruck, Gütersloh

PEFC-zertifiziert
Dieses Produkt stammt aus nachhaltig bewirtschafteten Wäldern und kontrollierten Quellen
PEFC/04-31-1033 www.pefc.de

ISBN: 978-3-06-123277-1 (Kursbuch)
Produktnummer: 1100034916 (E-Book)

TABLE OF CONTENTS

		TOPICS	LANGUAGE FUNCTIONS
	**1** **Socializing and small talk** Page 8	• Social interactions at work • First meetings • Small talk • Entertaining visitors	• Starting a conversation • Keeping a conversation going • Shifting the focus • Exchanging contact details
	**2** **Effective emails** Page 18	• Effective business writing • Inclusive language • Machine translation and AI	• Starting and ending an email • Getting your message across • Requesting action • Summarizing
	**3** **Who's calling?** Page 28	• Communication channels today • Phases of a voice or video call • Communication breakdown	• Paraphrasing and summarizing • Scheduling a phone call • Dealing with problems
	**4** **All in a day's work** Page 38	• Workplace interactions • Onboarding • Office design • Company events	• Showing people around • Describing and explaining • Expressing opinions
	**5** **Working together** Page 48	• The language of meetings • The language of internal presentations • Key performance indicators	• Facilitating meetings • Giving instructions tactfully • Reporting • Describing risks and challenges
	**6** **Global business speaks English** Page 58	• Effective use of English as a lingua franca • Meetings and presentations in a global context • Intercultural issues	• Checking understanding • Adapting your language • Navigating different communication styles

Partner Files	Page 68	**Useful Phrases**	Page 90
Transcripts	Page 74	**A-Z Wordlist**	Page 94
Answer Key	Page 82	**Key Verbs**	Page 96

INTRODUCING
ENGLISH FOR TODAY'S WORKPLACE

As you will have experienced in your own jobs, far-reaching transformations are taking place in the way we work. Among other things, hybrid working, decentralized and project-based roles and the increasing use of English as the preferred language of communication have become the norm. Some changes to our working models have evolved over years, some have accelerated over a short period of time and some, like the impact of artificial intelligence for example, are still to be felt.

While covering a broad range of situations and interactions which are relevant in any workplace, *English for Today's Workplace* pinpoints the aspects that have changed or are changing and presents the language we need to deal with them. This book is not designed to be industry-specific so it is suitable for use wherever you work. It will provide you with the communicative language skills which are vital for achieving results at work with co-workers, business partners and customers.

Reflecting the widespread use of English as a lingua franca in international business communication, *English for Today's Workplace* helps you to develop awareness and sensitivity towards different accents, varieties of English and cultural differences in communication style. This also includes awareness of your own English and strategies for being an effective communicator in a lingua franca context.

English for Today's Workplace contains the following components designed to help you learn effectively.

- The book's six units focus on a comprehensive range of key topics in line with the changing demands of today's workplace. As you can see from the table of contents on page 3, the aim is to give an overview of what you need to know in a compact format. The units have been written to be used in any order to suit your needs and priorities.

- ▷ U6: In Units 1 – 3, this icon in the margin with "U6" indicates that the topic of the exercise is picked up again in Unit 6 in a more explicitly intercultural context.

- Each unit includes all of the following features: warm-up activities to get you talking, language focus features to practise useful grammar and language structures, post-its as a quick reminder of possible pitfalls and useful information, vocabulary support and useful phrases you can use in language exercises and discussions as well as simulations and mediation activities which give you the opportunity to draw on your personal experience while practising key language.

- Simulations give you the opportunity to discuss or carry out a business task using your own life / work experience and personal approach to the issue in hand. They encourage you to use and adapt the language learned to perform tasks as you would in the real world.

- Mediation means helping people to communicate. In work-related contexts this may range from translating from one language to another, rephrasing, paraphrasing and summarizing within the same language, to explaining cultural differences in language use and behaviour. The mediation tasks in the book reflect what we do every day in our increasingly multicultural and multilingual business world.

- 🔊 There are listening tasks in every unit which enable you to hear speakers from many different language backgrounds using English in typical work situations. This broad range of listening tasks offers the opportunity to practise different skills, from listening for gist, listening for specific information and decoding speech to awareness of features of different accents. The recordings can be accessed using the **Cornelsen Lernen App** or the **webcode "pecaxe"** on **codes.cornelsen.de**.

- Each unit builds up to a final output section called Over To You. This is a partner or group task which enables you to use the language and ideas presented in the unit to deal with common business situations. The task concludes with a debriefing session encouraging you to evaluate your performance.

- The appendix provides partner files, transcripts of the audio recordings, an answer key, a collection of useful phrases, an A-Z wordlist as a summary of the vocabulary boxes in the units and a list of key verbs for your job. It is designed to help you to use the book in your own time as a resource for independent learning and for reference purposes.

- 👆 In addition to the recordings, the **Cornelsen Lernen App** offers interactive exercises, which practise and expand on the useful phrases provided in this book. They are designed as a resource for independent learning.

Before you start the English course, it's a good idea to reflect on and identify the gap between your existing language skills and knowledge and what you want to achieve. The Needs Analysis questionnaire on pages 6 and 7 will support you in setting personal learning goals at the outset and assessing your progress once you have worked through the book.

We hope you enjoy learning how to communicate more effectively at work with *English for Today's Workplace* and wish you every success.

Angela Lloyd
and the Cornelsen editorial team

NEEDS ANALYSIS

English for Today's Workplace is designed to provide practice to help you deal confidently with the challenge of using English in professional interactions. Technological developments, the increase in remote working, workplace diversity and the need to focus on inclusive language all lead to new demands on linguistic and social skills.

Before you start your English course, consider the following questions:
- Who do I communicate with? (co-workers, customers, first or second language speakers of English, team colleagues I rarely meet face-to-face, etc.)
- What channels of communication do I use? (emails, phone calls, instant messages, etc.)
- Where do I interact with others? (in online meetings, in person, in informal situations, etc.)
- What are the biggest language and communication challenges that I face?
- What are the biggest intercultural challenges that I face?

Use this needs analysis to help you make the most of your English course and maximize your learning. Look at the table below with the topic areas covered in this book and spend a few minutes thinking about the tasks that you most commonly do. Tick your personal priorities and current learning objectives. Add any other skills which are also relevant for you. Keep the skills which you find most challenging in mind while you are working on each unit of the book.

		need more practice / have made good progress
Tasks at the workplace		
Interacting socially at work	Meeting someone for the first time	☐ ☐
	Keeping a conversation going	☐ ☐
	Building rapport	☐ ☐
	Making small talk	☐ ☐
	_____	☐ ☐
	_____	☐ ☐
Communicating in writing	Getting my message across	☐ ☐
	Setting an appropriate tone in emails	☐ ☐
	Using inclusive language	☐ ☐
	Getting to the point in emails	☐ ☐
	_____	☐ ☐
	_____	☐ ☐
Using a telephone at work	Transitioning from small talk to business	☐ ☐
	Checking understanding	☐ ☐
	Passing on phone messages	☐ ☐
	Scheduling a phone call	☐ ☐
	_____	☐ ☐
	_____	☐ ☐

Tasks at the workplace

Interacting in the workplace
- Expressing my opinion clearly
- Giving instructions tactfully
- Showing a visitor around my company
- Describing a process or policy
- _____
- _____

Working in teams
- Checking and clarifying what people say
- Encouraging others to participate
- Keeping a meeting on track
- Giving project updates
- _____
- _____

Working across cultures
- Making what I say easy to understand
- Saying that I don't understand
- Presenting to an international audience
- Adapting to different communication styles
- _____
- _____

(columns: need more practice | have made good progress)

Once you have completed the units, assess your progress in each of the skills you ticked at the beginning of the course. Now tick the boxes which show where you have made good progress and where you need more practice.

Looking back at your answers to the questions on the previous page, make a note of your main takeaways from the book. What language input and tips did you find most useful?

Professional language and communication skills:

_____

_____

Intercultural skills:

_____

_____

Knowing what you already do well and what you could do better will allow you to focus on how you can consolidate what you have learned and improve the skills you really need.

THIS UNIT LOOKS AT ...
- the impact of workplace changes on how people communicate
- language we can use to interact socially at work

1 Socializing and small talk

 Read some comments about socializing at work and discuss what is true for you.

A I really feel that I'm out of practice at socializing with our customers and business partners. I often don't know what to talk about anymore!

B Companies have cut down on business trips so when visitors come, we make sure that we have plenty of time to socialize with them.

C After we changed from face-to-face to online meetings, we used to begin with some small talk but now we tend to just say hello and get on with the job.

D I've noticed that people socialize a lot more at work than they used to. We come in for trainings, presentations, lunches. We work at home and socialize at work!

 1 When do you have most of your informal conversations at work now? Rank the options, adding your own ideas if possible. Compare your answers with a partner.

- during telephone calls with clients
- in online meetings with my project team
- with my colleagues during a lunch or coffee break
- when greeting business visitors on arrival
- when taking visitors out to lunch or dinner
- at the beginning or end of face-to-face meetings
- while networking at conferences or trade fairs
- at company (social) events like office parties or staff meetings

> **LANGUAGE FOCUS**
>
> **Talking about changes in past habits**
> Use *used to + infinitive* to talk about past situations which are no longer true.
> *We used to meet face-to-face every week but now we meet online.*
>
> Use *never + past tense verb* in negative sentences.
> *Before we started working from home, we never had our meetings online.*
>
> Use *did you use to + infinitive* to ask about any changes.
> *Did you really use to have a two-hour journey to work every day?*

8 ENGLISH FOR TODAY'S WORKPLACE

2 Have you ever been unsure of what to say in English when you meet someone for the first time? Talk about your experience in the following situations.

1. knowing how to greet them
2. introducing yourself and other people
3. knowing how to address them after the introduction (first/last names, titles, etc.)
4. making them feel welcome and comfortable
5. saying you didn't understand something
6. adapting what you say if the first meeting is online

3 Listen and write the number of each conversation next to the correct picture.

A Conversation

B Conversation

C Conversation

D Conversation

4 Listen again and write in the missing verbs.

1. You _____ be Lena Seitz.
2. Can I _____ you a coffee or something else to drink?
3. I'd like to give Alessandro the chance to _____ who's who in the project team.
4. We're _____ to working with you.
5. I'm sorry, I didn't quite _____ the number.
6. Sorry to _____ you waiting.
7. I don't think we've _____ before.
8. Am I _____ your name correctly?

5 Which sentence in exercise 4 is used to …

a. make the visitor feel comfortable?
b. check understanding?
c. apologize?
d. start a conversation with a stranger?
e. show what the speaker thinks is true?
f. clarify something?
g. introduce the team to a newcomer?
h. welcome a new team member?

A good way to memorize people's names is to use them as soon as possible in your conversation.

UNIT 1: SOCIALIZING AND SMALL TALK

LANGUAGE FOCUS

Guessing something is true
We can use *must* to give an opinion based on things we know or can see. It is also a way to build a relationship by showing interest.
- *You must be Lena.* (I've heard about you.)
- *He must be very busy.* (I want to show understanding.)
- *You must remember Matt.* (He gave that entertaining presentation last year.)
- *Everyone must be very hungry.* (I know we're behind schedule.)

6 What would you say? Make up any details and share your ideas in class.

1 Your boss is taking an important video call which will take about half-an-hour. She asks you to go to reception to meet a new client from India.
2 You're making yourself a coffee in the office kitchen when a new English-speaking colleague, who you would like to get to know, comes in.
3 You're at the airport to pick up a business partner. The flight is two hours late and you have been waiting for a long time. You know the visitor quite well.

 7 We use small talk in informal conversations to break the ice and build rapport with others. Look at a list of potential topics and share your own experience with a partner by completing the sentences.

family | films/TV | food | health | home | music | mutual acquaintances | pets | politics | sport | topical issues in the news | travel | weekend | work situation

1 I would talk to a client about …
2 I would never talk about … because the topic bores me.
3 … is a good topic for a conversation with co-workers.
4 It's best to avoid controversial topics like …
5 I would never ask any questions about someone's … . I think it's very personal.
6 A topic like … is OK to start a conversation, but you need to move on to something else quickly.

VOCABULARY

to **bore so** jmdn. langweilen
controversial strittig, brisant
mutual acquaintances gemeinsame Bekannte

8 Match the questions and answers.

1 You're a marathon runner, right?
2 How often do you get back to Spain?
3 Did you have any problems getting here?
4 How's the project going?
5 How difficult is it to find a flat in Paris?
6 Did you watch the match on TV last night?

a Very well. We have a great team.
b Unfortunately I did. And my team lost again!
c Why? Are you planning to move there?
d Oh yes! The next one is in Berlin in September.
e Not as often as I would like.
f There were no delays at all so I got here very quickly.

ENGLISH FOR TODAY'S WORKPLACE

9 Read some excerpts from informal conversations. Which of the topics from exercise 7 are they talking about?

1 "It's not easy to find the time, but I find getting out and kicking a ball around is a great way to relax."
2 "Well, they're all grown up now."
3 "I haven't got anything booked yet, but it will be nice to get away."
4 "It's a lovely spot – very quiet, with beautiful views. We've been there for seven years."
5 "If you used to work in the Munich office, you must know Peter Meyer."
6 "I work such long hours during the week that I just relax most of the time!"

Work with a partner and write a short dialogue which includes one of the excerpts.

10 Follow the instructions to role play three small talk conversations. In each conversation, one partner plays themselves and the other partner plays the chosen role. Choose suitable small talk topic(s) for each situation.

> Many topics are not necessarily good or bad for small talk. It depends on who you are talking to, how well you know them and where you are having the conversation.

1 Pick one option from each box to create a role. Start small talking!
2 Cross out the options chosen in 1. Pick different options to create a new role for a new conversation.
3 Cross out the options chosen in 2. Role play a conversation with the remaining options.

person	age	relationship	place
business partner	25–35	know each other well	company cafeteria
co-worker	36–46	met once or twice before	networking event
visitor	47–60	first meeting	reception area

Share the choices you and your partner made to create the roles and explain the topics you talked about.

11 Listen and tick in which version the speaker sounds more interested in the conversation. Rising intonation ↑ sounds more positive than falling intonation ↓.

1 A B   2 A B   3 A B

> To keep a conversation going, especially with someone you don't yet know very well, be interesting in what you say and – even more important – sound interested in what your partner is saying!

LANGUAGE FOCUS

Open and closed questions

We often start a conversation with a closed question and then continue with open, follow-up questions to keep the conversation going.

- Closed questions can be answered with *yes* or *no* or a short phrase.
  Do you live in London? | Did you miss the train? | Was the conference interesting?
- Open questions often begin with a question word (*why, how, what*) or a phrase like *What's your opinion of ….? | What happened next?*

Did you have a good journey? – No, unfortunately not! – Oh no, what happened?

UNIT 1: SOCIALIZING AND SMALL TALK

12 Choose two possible ways to continue each conversation.

1 Do you still live in Madrid (or another city)? – Yes, I do. – …
2 Are you watching that new TV series everyone's talking about? – Yes, I am in fact. – …
3 Is the project going well? – No, not at all, unfortunately. – …
4 Are you interested in sport? – Not really, to be honest. – …

a Really? What's gone wrong?
b How long are you planning to stay there?
c So, what are you going to do now?
d What do you think of the actors?
e So, how do you usually spend your free time?
f Same with me! So, what interests you more?
g What are the most interesting things to do there?
h What do you think will happen in the next episode?

Choose one of the conversations and continue it. See how long you can keep talking.

13 Helen and Alessandro are on a video call. Read part of their conversation and mark the 3As as shown on the post-it on the right.

Helen: By the way, Alessandro, I've been meaning to ask you this – did you move to Milan to start your new job?
Alessandro: No, I didn't. I've always lived in Milan. Have you ever been here?
Helen: Yes, twice in fact. We had our project kick-off meeting there. I really loved the city. In fact, that was one of the very few face-to-face team meetings we've had. How do you like having most meetings online?
Alessandro: Well, I like it. This way we speak with each other often. But you know, Helen, maybe you liked Milan so much because you met the whole team in person?
Helen: Well, yes, you might be right! But it is a great city, isn't it?
Alessandro: Of course – no question! But coming back to your question about meeting online – what's your opinion?
Helen: I like it, too. As you say, we speak often so we work together very effectively this way. Let's get started, shall we?

The 3As of balanced conversation are Answer your partner, Add another piece of information, Ask another question.

14 Find out what schmoozing is by completing the explanation with words from the box.

| communicating | importantly | interested | listening | name | relationships | remember | schmoozers |

Schmoozing is a way of _____¹ with people in order to develop _____². The best _____³ listen carefully and, most _____⁴, use phrases to show that they are _____⁵ to you and are _____⁶ in your opinions. They often repeat your _____⁷ during a conversation and show that they _____⁸ facts about you.

To schmooze is informal American English.

Read the conversation in exercise 13 again and find examples of how Helen and Alessandro use schmoozing techniques to communicate

ENGLISH FOR TODAY'S WORKPLACE

Decide on a topic you would like to talk about (small talk or work-related). Use the 3As to keep your conversation going and schmoozing techniques to show your interest in the topic and your partner's opinions.

> **USEFUL PHRASES**
>
> **Shifting the focus in a conversation**
>
> - OK then everyone, shall we make a start?
> - Right, if everyone's finished their coffee, let's get started.
> - It's 11.30 already, so shall we start the meeting?
> - Well, we have a lot on the agenda for today so I think it's time to start.
> - We have a new team member so let's start with a round of introductions.
> - Anyway, there's something I'd like to ask you about the project schedule.
> - Well, I suppose now would be a good time to look at latest sales figures.

We often use "so", "right", "well", "well ... so", "anyway", "OK then" to signal that we want to move on to a new topic. Remember to sound friendly and positive when you use these expressions.

15 Small talk helps to create a positive atmosphere but, at some point, you need to get down to business. Practise making this transition with your partner.

Partner Files, File 1: Partner A, page 68 | Partner B, page 71

16 Read how members of a cross-functional project team talk about their responsibilities. Use the underlined expressions to tell the group about your own position in your company.

Giulia: <u>I'm responsible for</u> managing the project so <u>I oversee</u> the day-to-day functioning of the project and <u>look for ways to</u> increase efficiency.
Alessandro: <u>I'm in charge of</u> our marketing strategy.
Matt: <u>I'm concerned with</u> securing new customers.
Helen: <u>I'm a</u> software developer <u>so it's my job to deliver</u> working software whenever we need it.
Amira: <u>I'm from</u> HR <u>so I make sure</u> we don't lose sight of personnel issues.
Piotr: I <u>work in</u> finance <u>so I focus on</u> the bottom line.

*Watch out for **false friends**!*

*to **oversee** sth/so = etw./jmdn. betreuen*
*to **overlook** sth/so = etw./jmdn. übersehen*

personnel = Personal
personal = persönlich

> **VOCABULARY**
>
> **the bottom line** Nettoergebnis, Endresultat
> **cross-functional** funktionsübergreifend
> to **lose sight of sth/so** *hier:* etw./jmdn. vernachlässigen
> to **oversee sth/so** etw./jmdn. betreuen
> to **secure sth** *hier:* etw. gewinnen

17 Imagine you are in an elevator with a new business contact. How would you introduce yourself and your job responsibilities in 30 seconds?

Prepare your elevator speech and introduce yourself to your partner.

18 Do businesses still need printed business cards? Talk about their role in your business environment by discussing to what extent the following comments reflect your experience and opinion.

> In my job, having printed business cards is essential. We work with industrial partners in Japan and South Korea and they certainly expect it. It's useful to be able to refer to the cards when we sit down to talk. To me, they are also the easiest way of sharing contact details at any networking events.
>
> Rodrigo

> I no longer use printed business cards. During the pandemic, when there were no face-to-face meetings and conferences, exchanging cards stopped. I only use virtual cards because they can be shared so easily. Online meeting platforms let you have a QR code next to your name so everyone has immediate access to your contact details anyway. It's so much more efficient!
>
> Verena

Dexter

> Digital networking has made it easy to exchange contact information, but I see printed cards as an essential part of my marketing toolkit. To me, a well-designed card is a great way to make a positive first impression. It reflects the professionalism, creativity and attention to detail which make our brand what it is today.

Look at the expressions in the Useful Phrases box and exchange your own contact details in class.

USEFUL PHRASES   Exchanging contact details

Offering printed cards
1. May I give you my card?
2. Shall we exchange contact details? Here's my card.
3. Here are my contact details if you have a query.
4. By the way, here's my card. Don't hesitate to contact me.

Offering virtual contact details
1. I'll send you a connection request now via social media. I'm sure you use this app. What's your full name?
2. Would you like to share your contact details?
3. I'll send you my digital card by email.

Responding
– Thank you. Here's mine.
– Great, thanks. Oh no, I've run out of cards. Can I give you my email address instead?
– Thanks. Let me give you my card.
– Thanks. I'll be in touch.

– Yes, I do. My name is Chris Price.

– Sure. Just scan my digital card. Here's the QR code.
– I have a card in my email signature, too.

ENGLISH FOR TODAY'S WORKPLACE

19 Entertaining business visitors usually involves eating together. Tick the statements you agree with. Discuss your opinions in class.

A There's nothing wrong with taking visitors to the canteen for lunch. It's quicker and less expensive. After a big lunch at a restaurant, everyone is too tired to work effectively.

B Taking business partners from East Asia to the canteen doesn't seem appropriate so ordering finger food from a catering service for lunch and eating out in the evening is a better idea.

C We just offer snacks and refreshments during our meetings. Most participants prefer to have a shorter lunch break and travel home from the meeting as early as possible.

D Choosing a suitable restaurant can be difficult. Some visitors are keen to try German food, but some are rather reluctant! To be on the safe side, it's a good idea to check if they have any dietary needs or specific likes and dislikes.

E Inviting clients and business partners to your home in the evening is a great way to show you value the relationship. It doesn't have to be a formal dinner – a casual get-together is fine.

VOCABULARY

appropriate angemessen
casual zwanglos
dietary needs Ernährungsanforderungen
get-together Beisammensein, Treffen
to involve sth etw. beinhalten
reluctant widerwillig, zurückhaltend
suitable geeignet
to value sth/so etw./jmdn. wertschätzen

Describe how your company or your department organizes meals and eating out for different kinds of business visitors.

20 Listen to three conversations and match each one to a location.

A Conversation

B Conversation

C Conversation

*In the restaurant, Lauren uses **gender-neutral language**. She asks the server (not waiter / waitress) to recommend a dish and refers to the person as they (not him / her).*

VOCABULARY

ingredient Zutat
signature dish Spezialität des Hauses
spicy food scharfes Essen
vegetarian vegetarisch, Vegetarier*in

UNIT 1: SOCIALIZING AND SMALL TALK

21 Listen again and complete the sentences you hear.

1 I think it's _____ to have something to eat.
2 The plates of vegetarian and vegan food are _____.
3 It's a good idea to have _____ so we don't all fall asleep this afternoon!
4 Don't bother reading the menu – just come and _____.
5 This is what's _____ today. All the food is halal, by the way.
6 I'm not very hungry so can I ask for _____?
7 The trays are _____.
8 By the way, do either of you have any _____?
9 What would you _____, Lauren?
10 The _____ at this restaurant is an Argentinian specialty.
11 What are _____, Lauren?
12 So, how _____? Was everything all right?
13 So, _____ a dessert?
14 I really _____ another mouthful.

> It's a good idea to check how words are pronounced in English, especially if they seem very similar to their German translations. Did you notice how these words are pronounced in English in the conversations?
> allergies | dessert | halal | vegan | vegetarian

 22 MEDIATION

Imagine your English-speaking visitors have asked you to explain the German and Austrian dishes they have found on the menu on the right. What would you say? Use the vague language expressions in the Useful Phrases box if you aren't sure how to explain. Compare your ideas in class.

Soljanka mit Zitronenscheibe und Sahnehäubchen

Rheinischer Sauerbraten mit Rotkohl und Kartoffelklößen

Labskaus mit Rollmops, Rote Beete und Spiegelei

Kaiserschmarrn mit Apfelmus oder Zwetschgenröster

USEFUL PHRASES

Vague language

- As far as I know, it's a kind of …
- This is a traditional dish from …
- It tastes a bit like …
- Actually, I have no idea what … is.
- I would guess from the name that it's …
- It's a sort of …
- I suppose it's a type of …
- I'm not sure what's in it, but it's delicious.
- It looks like … but in fact …
- I've never eaten anything like that myself.

23 Which restaurant in your area would you take visitors to your company? Remember to think about any potential dietary needs. Tell your partner and describe some of its best dishes. Use a dictionary to check any vocabulary you are not sure of.

OVER TO YOU

1 In his famous book *How to Win Friends and Influence People* (published in 1936), Dale Carnegie suggested six principles. Read what he wrote and discuss how useful they are for socializing effectively in your business environment today.

> Principle 1 – Become genuinely interested in other people.
> Principle 2 – Smile.
> Principle 3 – Remember that a person's name is to that person the sweetest and most important sound in any language.
> Principle 4 – Be a good listener. Encourage others to talk about themselves.
> Principle 5 – Talk in terms of the other person's interests.
> Principle 6 – Make the other person feel important - and do it sincerely.

2 Think about the following questions and make notes of your answers.

1. Who do you (or will you) have informal conversations with in English as part of your job? How much do you know about them?
2. Why do you meet them / talk to them?
3. What topics of conversation are suitable / unsuitable?
4. Where do (will) these conversations usually take place?
5. What information do you give about yourself?

3 SIMULATION

Based on the notes you both made, create a scenario for your meeting which is as realistic as possible for your own work situation.

1 Agree on a situation.
- What are your roles?
- Do you already know each other (e.g. in-person or only online)?
- Where are you meeting (e.g. airport, office foyer, conference)?
- Why are you meeting / having a conversation?

2 Check the language you will need.
Look back through the unit to find useful language for the stages of a conversation.
Read through the audio transcripts on pages 74 and 75 to find more phrases you can use.

3 Simulate the situation – Partner A is the host, Partner B is the visitor.
- Introduce yourselves.
- Start a conversation with some small talk.
- Remember to use the 3As to keep the conversation going.
- Make the transition from small talk to business talk.

4 Debriefing
- Did you manage to keep the conversation going?
- Was the atmosphere positive and friendly?
- Did you speak English confidently?
- Would you do anything differently in a real-life interaction?

> A *debriefing* session at the end of a project gives the team the chance to discuss what went well and what improvements they can make next time.

UNIT 1: SOCIALIZING AND SMALL TALK

2 Effective emails

THIS UNIT LOOKS AT ...
- choosing the most suitable phrases for your email
- how to use gender-neutral language
- using modern technology for written communication

Read what Susil says about how she spends an average working day and complete bar chart B so it is true for you.

My Working Day
WORKPLACES TODAY

by Susil Budi

In the past, in my job as an IT Manager for the German subsidiary of a multinational company, I used to spend a lot of time with the clients, on their premises. Now, I work from home most of the time so face-to-face meetings are rare – maybe once every two to four weeks. Apart from having online meetings (with customers, weekly internal meetings, update meetings), I communicate a lot more in writing as you can see from the chart. I start the day by reading emails and answering the urgent ones. At the end of the day, I spend time writing emails to let everyone know what has been done and what the next step will be – and I write and revise the documentation of our meetings. I rarely phone my boss – I send her emails instead so she can answer in her own time.

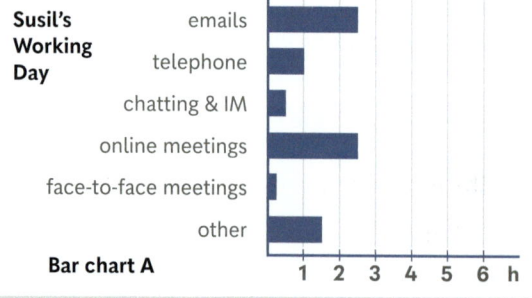

Bar chart A

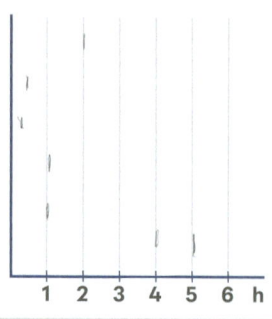

Bar chart B

 Present your bar chart to a partner, focusing mainly on the time you spend on writing tasks. Discuss whether you communicate more by email now than in the past.

VOCABULARY

(business) premises (pl.) Geschäftsräume, Betriebsgebäude
subsidiary Niederlassung, Tochterunternehmen

1 Read Aaron's blogpost on business writing and cross out the incorrect words in the examples he mentions.

The nuts and bolts of effective business writing

October 16th, posted by Aaron Butler

For your business writing to make a professional impression, you must get the basics right. Although everyone has access to spelling and grammar checkers, you'd be surprised at the number of mistakes I see in emails and text messages, whether they are written by people who have English as their first language or not. Of course, some errors may only be typos, but this means the writer didn't proofread before pressing send. So, here's my challenge for you today – can you get it right first time?

Their / There / They're waiting for you in the car park.

Many *company's / companies* have premises in the new industrial park.

Who's / Whose turn is it to write the minutes of the meeting today?

Unfortunately, *its / it's* still not clear what caused the problem.

Is that coffee mine or *your's / yours*?

Discuss the following questions in class.

1 Do you get work emails – in any language – which contain mistakes?
2 Do you ever notice too late that you have made mistakes? Why does this happen and what can you do about it?

VOCABULARY

minutes (of a meeting) Protokoll
the nuts and bolts die praktischen Grundlagen
to proofread sth etw. Korrektur lesen
typo Tippfehler

LANGUAGE FOCUS Email greetings

1 If a person has more than one title, only use the highest one in English, however formal the email is: *Dear Dr Preier (Ms Dr Preier)* or *Dear Professor Wilms (Mr. Professor Dr. Wilms)*
2 A comma can but does not have to be placed between certain greetings and the name:
Hi, Carlos ... / Hello Mireia ... / Good morning, Mr Coessens
3 In **American English** a comma is usually placed after the name, but in a very formal email a colon is used: *Dear Dr. / Mr. / Ms. Smith, ...* or *Dear Mr. Smith: ...*
In **British English** the greeting can be written with or without a comma:
Dear Dr / Mr / Ms Smith or *Dear Dr / Mr / Ms Smith, ...*

2 Look at the opening greetings below and mark them as follows: F (formal), N (neutral), I (informal).

Good morning, Philip	Dear Jane Anderson	Hi, Jessica
Dear colleagues	Hi, everyone	Dear all,
Hello, Véronique	Dear Sir/Madam	Stephan

Thinking about your own recent work email contacts, which opening greetings would be most suitable when writing to each of them in English?

Remember that the first sentence in an email always begins with a capital letter, even if the opening greeting ends with a comma or a colon.

LANGUAGE FOCUS

Using gender-neutral opening greetings in emails

The goal of gender-neutral language is to connect in an inclusive way with the people you are writing to. In a business context ...

first name / given name Vorname
family name / surname Nachname
Note: In the case of East Asian names, the first name is the family name, followed by the given name.

1 ... you may be writing to someone you have never met and do not know the gender of the person because the name is unfamiliar to you or is gender-neutral.
For example, Turkish first names are not always specifically male or female so you may meet people of different genders with the same first name.

2 ... even if you know that the name is male or female, you may not know whether the person identifies as female, male or non-binary.

3 ... you may be writing to a diverse group.

Tips

- When writing to a person whose name you know, use **Dear + given name**, **Dear + full name** (a good idea if you are not sure which name is the family name) or **Dear + initials + family name**.
- Use **Dear Mx + family name** (instead of Mr, Mrs, Ms). Only use this if you know that the person wishes to be addressed in a gender-neutral way.
- If the name is unknown, use the position: **Dear Manager**, **Dear Customer**, **Dear Helpline**
- When writing to a group, there are many possibilities: **Dear team, Dear all, Dear colleagues**, etc.
- **Good morning, Greetings, Hello**, etc. are possible opening greetings if you don't know the name of the person.

If your own name may not be easily recognizable as male or female to business partners or if you wish to be addressed in gender-neutral language, include your own pronouns in your email signature after your name:
Deniz Özdemir (she/her) or (they/them/their)

3 Using *they* as a singular pronoun is a gender-neutral way of referring to other people in an email. Complete the sentences without using gender-related pronouns (*he/his*, etc.).

1 In _____ email to me, Maher asked for details of our sales campaign.

2 I enjoyed Ümit's talk. _____ always have something interesting to say.

3 When our new intern joined the team, I briefed _____ on the status of the project.

*They used as a singular pronoun was named Word of the Year 2019 by the Merriam-Webster Dictionary. In fact, using **they** to refer to one person (but with a plural verb) goes back to the 14th century.*

ENGLISH FOR TODAY'S WORKPLACE

4 Javid, a communications trainer, has their own podcast. Listen to them talking about writing effective emails and make a note of the six points they mention.

> **VOCABULARY**
>
> **accuracy** sprachliche Richtigkeit
> **artificial intelligence (AI)** künstliche Intelligenz (KI)
> **confidential** vertraulich
> **machine translation** maschinelle Übersetzung
> to **rely on sth** sich auf etw. verlassen

5 Listen again and, with a partner, use your notes and the phrases below to discuss Javid's tips and what you need to do to improve your own email writing in English.

I agree with the part(s) about …

One of my tips for writing good emails is …

I'd never really thought about … before, but …

I'd like to know more about …

I'm not sure if I agree with the idea of …

6 Read some suggestions for email openers and match each one with the message it sends the reader.

The writer …

1 I hope this finds you well.
2 Thank you for your excellent suggestion in the online meeting yesterday.
3 How have you been since we last spoke?
4 I know how busy you are, so I'll be brief.
5 I hope the Greek project is going smoothly. Do let me know if you need any help.
6 I'm writing to send you the information you requested in your email.
7 Thanks for getting back to me so quickly with the sales figures.
8 I was so pleased that we were able to meet up again last week.

a … doesn't want to waste my time.
b … asks a friendly question to show interest in me.
c … refers to an email I sent and introduces the topic of this one.
d … uses a very standard beginning.
e … gives me positive feedback.
f … says the writer appreciates my work.
g … shows interest in my work.
h … refers to a personal connection between us.

7 Look at some reasons for writing an email and choose an appropriate phrase (1–8) which reflects the purpose of the email.

apologizing | complaining | following up | informing | inviting | providing documentation | requesting | thanking

1 I would like to ask you to send me the signed contract by June 4th. _____
2 I really appreciated your help in getting the project off to a good start. _____
3 I am pleased to announce that management has agreed to our request. _____
4 As requested, please find attached the draft contract and guidelines. _____
5 I am afraid that we are not at all happy with the quality of your last delivery. _____
6 I am writing to you in connection with our meeting in Vienna two weeks ago. _____
7 We are very sorry for the inconvenience caused by our late delivery. _____
8 I would like to welcome you to join us for a presentation of our new procurement guidelines. _____

Now look at three more opening sentences and discuss whether the reason for writing is immediately clear to the reader. If not, why not? Discuss with your partner how you could rephrase each sentence.

1 You still haven't sent me the price list I asked for.
2 I would appreciate it if you could find time to meet me next week.
3 I'm writing with regard to yesterday's meeting.

8 Complete these opening phrases in ways which reflect your own work.

1 I am pleased to announce that _____
2 Unfortunately, we are not at all happy with _____
3 As requested, please find attached _____
4 I am writing to you in connection with _____
5 I would be grateful if you could _____
6 We are very sorry for _____

9 Compare the closing remarks you usually write (in German or another language) in an email before you sign off. Decide which are standard phrases and which are personal remarks and discuss what you would write in English in each case.

10 Check the signing off phrases below and mark the four most informal endings. What equivalent in German can you think of for each of the phrases? Compare your ideas with a partner.

| ☐ Sincerely | ☐ Best wishes | ☐ Kind regards | ☐ Regards | ☐ Cheers |
| ☐ Take care | ☐ (your name) | ☐ All the best | ☐ Best | ☐ Yours |

ENGLISH FOR TODAY'S WORKPLACE

11 Complete these closing remarks with phrases from the box.

day off | keep me informed | don't hesitate | for the weekend | how it went | your thoughts |
if you need any input | a good time | hearing | say "Hi" | my fingers crossed | on the project

1 If you have any further questions, please _____ to contact me.
2 I look forward to _____ from you.
3 Please _____ if anything changes with regard to the planning.
4 Just give me a call _____ from our side.
5 Any plans _____?
6 I'll keep _____ that your presentation goes well!
7 Enjoy your _____!
8 Looking forward to working with you _____.
9 Please let me know _____ on this matter.
10 Please let me know when it would be _____ to call you.
11 Don't forget to _____ to Renzo from me.
12 Have a good holiday. I'll be interested to hear _____.

Watch out!
I look forward to hear**ing** from you.
I look forward to meet**ing** you next week.
I look forward to work**ing** with you on the new project.

Which of these closing remarks and which of the signing off phrases in exercise 10 do you or would you use in your work emails?

12 Match pairs of sentences with the same meaning from two emails. Now decide which is the more formal [F] and the more informal [I] version in each case.

1 Thanks for your heads up about the meeting next week.
2 I can make it.
3 I very much look forward to seeing you next week.
4 If you think it's appropriate, I'll ask Sophia to attend in her place.
5 Unfortunately Anna will be unable to attend.
6 Great to hear from you.
7 I'd be very grateful for further details about the other participants.
8 I must apologize for not replying sooner.

a I thought I'd ask Sophia to come instead. What do you think?
b Anna can't come.
c Sorry, I haven't got back to you sooner.
d Thank you very much for informing me of the upcoming meeting.
e Who else is going to be there?
f See you next week, then!
g I'd like to confirm that I will attend.
h I was very pleased to receive your email.

Write each complete email, putting the sentences in the correct order. Discuss which style is closer to most of the work emails you send and receive. Does your company provide style guides or models?

13 What impact could the following aspects have on the tone and style of business emails? Consider the comments, add your own ideas and give some examples.

content | culture | frequency of communication | reason for writing | relationship between writer and recipient | urgency

> **VOCABULARY**
> **businesslike** sachlich
> **frequency** Häufigkeit
> **recipient** Empfänger*in
> **reserved** zurückhaltend
> **urgency** Dringlichkeit

In a series of back-and-forth emails with a team colleague, the style always changes to save time.

Every time I receive a badly written email, I realize how important it is to get the tone and style right in my own emails.

I don't use just one email style – it depends who I'm writing to.

Read the emails and make notes on the tone (friendly, businesslike, reserved) and style (formal, neutral, informal) of each one and why you think they were written like this.

Dear Mr Austin,
Further to our conversation yesterday, I would like to inform you that a meeting with our specialist for tax law has been scheduled for next Wednesday, July 2nd at 11:30 at our office. Please do not hesitate to contact me if you require any further information before the meeting.
Yours sincerely,
Barbara Young

1 _____

Cristina,
As we discussed this morning, please send your list of questions to Mike and Pavel without delay. You'll find everything you need to consider in the attachment. We need their input before we can move forward.
Josephine

2 _____

Hi, Jorge,
How was your weekend? Did you manage to get away as planned? I hope so.
Anyway, I'm writing to ask if you could send me an update on the status of the construction work. Elena keeps asking me for details! We can set up a call for later today if that would be more convenient for you.
Cheers.
Tim

3 _____

Dear all,
I am pleased to announce that after a successful testing phase our new dealership management system is scheduled to go live on March 1st, exactly as planned. This is excellent news.
Please find an overview of the test results in the attached file.
Thanks to you all for your collaboration, expert input and hard work.
Kind regards,
Michèle Girardin

4 _____

---

14 An email may often include a request for action. Look back at emails 2 and 3 above and find the phrases which request action from the recipient. How are they different?

ENGLISH FOR TODAY'S WORKPLACE

15 SIMULATION

Draft an email requesting action on an urgent matter. Make up any names and details as necessary.

1 Choose scenario A or B, or make up your own based on your work situation.

A You have an important meeting tomorrow with a client which you can't reschedule. Write to a co-worker to ask them to host a delegation from Poland in your place.
Send information about what has been planned for the visit. Tell them what to do if there are any problems.

B You have a project meeting the day after tomorrow to discuss the sales figures for commercial vehicles at the dealerships in your region. They will form the basis for some important decisions.
Write to the manager of the one dealership which hasn't yet submitted any data to ask for the figures.

2 Write a subject line, but check it again after you have written the email.
3 Decide which opening greeting to use and how to start your email. Choose the most suitable tone and style for the purpose of the email and your relationship with the recipient.
4 Start the email by clearly sharing the reason for writing. Include all necessary information.
5 Explain why the matter is urgent and ask the recipient to act. Use the phrases below to help you.
6 Choose suitable closing remarks and sign off.

> *Strong **subject lines** are short and focused and include keywords to make it easy to search for later. Avoid words that may sound like spam. Remember to update the subject line, if necessary, in an email chain.*

USEFUL PHRASES Requesting action on urgent matters

Requesting action
- I am writing to ask / remind you to …
- Please let me have …
- I need …
- Could you …?

Being diplomatic
- I'd like to ask you a favour. Could you …?
- I know you are busy, but …
- I look forward to receiving …

Expressing urgency
- This is a very urgent matter.
- Please … without further delay.
- We must solve this by tomorrow / asap.
- Please make this a priority.

Showing gratitude
- I would be grateful if you could help me out.
- Thanks in advance!
- This would be very helpful.

Debriefing

Before you start, look back at Javid's six points for writing effective emails (exercise 5).
Look critically at your email and discuss the following questions with your partner.

- Will the recipient know why they have received the email?
- Is the action point clear?
- Does the email have a clear beginning, middle and end?
- Did we proofread it carefully?

16   Mark the language aids you use at work. Discuss the questions with your partner.

☐ machine translation apps
☐ online dictionary
☐ AI-powered chatbots
☐ smartphone voice translator app
☐ digital translator
☐ print dictionary

1 Are any of the items above out-of-date now? Why do you think so?
2 Do you use machine translation apps to write work emails? If so, what kind of emails?
3 Do you use AI-powered chatbots to write emails (in any language) for you? If so, give some examples of the prompts you use.
4 Would you use a voice translator when you meet business partners from abroad face-to-face? Why/why not?

> **Prompts** are questions or instructions which users enter into a chatbot. Specific and carefully worded prompts get more suitable responses.

VOCABULARY

confident zuversichtlich
to **spot sth** etw. entdecken
straightforward einfach, unkompliziert
subject matter Materie, Thematik

17 (06) Listen to an episode of Javid's podcast on the topic of machine translation and AI-powered chatbots. Are the following statements true or false?

	True	False
1 Liliana uses a translation app to check the emails she writes to clients because she wants to sound professional.	☐	☐
2 Liliana thinks translation tools help her to take risks.	☐	☐
3 Eduardo uses AI chatbots to write emails because they save him a lot of time.	☐	☐
4 Although AI makes his life easier, Eduardo knows he still needs to improve his English.	☐	☐
5 Tobias would never use AI-based tools for emails.	☐	☐
6 Tobias wants to learn new words and phrases and improve his grammar.	☐	☐

18   Listen again and make notes on what they say. Summarize the benefits ☺ and drawbacks ☹ and discuss them with your partner, based on your own experience.

USEFUL PHRASES   Summarizing people's opinions

- Generally speaking, all of them think …
- On the whole, machine translation apps provide …
- … seem(s) to think that …
- They appear to agree that …
- One drawback seems to be that …
- The main benefits they mention are …

19   Will technology eliminate the need to learn other languages for work purposes? Discuss this question with your partner, then summarize your opinions for the class.

OVER TO YOU

 1 How could a translation app help you learn another language – and not just be a shortcut to writing an email or other document? Discuss this with your partner.

> **LANGUAGE FOCUS** Developing a simple, clear style of writing
>
> Good translation apps provide alternative ways of translating a sentence, often with the option of using a verb or a noun. To make your writing easier to read in English, …
>
> **1** … turn nouns – especially clusters of nouns as in this example – into verbs.
>
> *Our software will help in the development, implementation and evaluation of your training courses.*
> → *… will help you to develop, implement and evaluate your training courses.*
>
> **2** … turn the noun into a verb if the sentence includes verbs like "conduct", "give", "have" or "make" followed by a noun.
>
> *conduct an investigation* → *investigate* *have a meeting* → *meet*
> *give a description* → *describe* *make an arrangement* → *arrange*

2 Rewrite the sentences by replacing the underlined noun phrases with verbs, as in the example.

Example: May I <u>offer the suggestion</u> that we look for another supplier in Brazil?
 May I suggest that we look for another supplier in Brazil?

1 When we meet in June, we can <u>have a discussion</u> of our options.
2 To take part in the job-sharing programme, you need to <u>send an application</u> by January 30th.
3 So far this year, the company <u>has made savings of</u> € 150,000 on storage costs.
4 The <u>aim of</u> the project is <u>the standardization of</u> our transaction processes.
5 May I ask you to let me know any <u>recommendations</u> you would <u>make</u>?
6 Please <u>send a confirmation of</u> the date and time of our meeting next week.
7 Our <u>expectation</u> is that profits will remain stable over the next year.
8 We <u>have the intention</u> to increase our production capacity in the future.

 3 MEDIATION

 1 Bring two or three emails you have recently written in German to co-workers or clients to class. Now redraft these emails in English. Look back through the unit to find suitable phrases to get your message across.

 2 Exchange your redrafted emails with your partner and give each other feedback.

*Remember to **proofread** your emails before you send them – not just for errors in spelling and grammar but for tone and level of (in)formality. Keep to the same style throughout the email.*

THIS UNIT LOOKS AT ...
- how telephoning has changed
- phrases for different phases of a call
- the integration of different communication channels

3 Who's calling?

 Look at the potential uses of phones at work and add any others you can think of. Discuss which functions you use a lot and why you find them useful in your job.

> calendar management | camera | email | contact list | instant messaging | internet access | online meetings | video calls | voice calls | voicemail

 1 Telephony has changed radically in recent years with far-reaching effects on how we work. Read and discuss some comments on different aspects of these changes. What is true for you?

A I hardly ever use my phone to actually speak to people. I would guess that about 90% of the time we communicate via chats.

B The switch from landlines to a cloud-based VoIP phone system means that customers can reach me on my office number even though I'm at home or "on the road".

C My company takes data security very seriously so most staff have company-issued phones where access to certain social media platforms is banned.

D Chatting has made business communication more informal. In fact, I often use emojis in my messages – but not when I'm interacting with clients!

LANGUAGE FOCUS   It depends ...

If there is not one clear-cut answer to a question, we often start by saying: "It depends".
Look at more ways of using this very useful phrase.
- It depends on (the situation / the person).
- It depends on how (urgent it is / well I know the person).
- It depends on when / why (I need to talk).
- It depends on whether (I need someone to act fast).

VOCABULARY

banned untersagt
clear-cut eindeutig
company-issued firmeneigen
far-reaching weitreichend
on the road hier: unterwegs
a switch to sth ein Wechsel zu etw.
to switch to sth zu etw. wechseln

ENGLISH FOR TODAY'S WORKPLACE

2 Take turns to summarize the most important points of two voice or video calls you made recently. Tell your partner why you decided to speak rather than write to the recipient.

- We talked about …
- I wanted to tell … about …
- I needed to know if …
- The reason I phoned was because …

Read what Markus, an engineer from Cologne, says about his reasons for choosing to pick up the phone. Do you agree with him? Do you have anything to add?

> I don't speak on the phone as often as I used to, but there are times when it's essential. So, if we have an urgent problem to solve, I prefer to call someone, then I know they've received the information. If I only send a message or text, it might be overlooked. I also think it's important to speak to someone personally if I have bad news of any kind or want to apologize. In my opinion, that's one way of showing that the working relationship is important to me.

3 MEDIATION

Listen to a call from a customer with an urgent question. If you were Alena, what message would you give Sergio? How would you contact him (in-person, by phone, by email, etc.)? Work with a partner to draft a suitable message.

Partner A: Draft a message in German.

Partner B: Draft a message in English, using the language of paraphrasing and summarizing.

Compare your messages:
- Do both messages contain the same information?
- What differences are there in the language of the English and German messages?
  Think about the grammar and sentence structure and about the length of the text.

LANGUAGE FOCUS

Paraphrasing and summarizing information
When passing on information to others, it's not necessary to report the exact words which were spoken or written.
It's more effective to summarize the message, using reporting verbs.

Stating a fact
- Mr Barbato **phoned to complain** about the hotel you booked for him.
- Rosa **emailed me to confirm** that she's ready to send the report today.
- I **got a phone call to say that** the meeting has been cancelled.

Calling for action
- Vladimir **wants you to send** some more samples immediately!
- Mr Wu **suggests that** we redraft the contract before his visit.
- Sandrine **recommends that** you give her a call before the meeting.

Watch out!
fabric = Stoff (Textilerzeugnis)
factory = Fabrik

---

 4 Use the phrases in bold from the Language Focus to make statements which reflect what you might say while you're doing your job. Use past or present verbs as appropriate. Share your sentences in class.

5 Look at how business phone calls have evolved and match each situation described in the timeline to a suitable phrase (a-e).

1. The caller dials the switchboard of a company and is redirected to the person they want to speak to.
2. The caller sometimes has the option of using the person's direct line. Landline phones also have a caller display.
3. The sound quality and signal strength of mobile phones are not always very good.
4. The use of texting and instant messaging means callers can check if it is convenient before making the call.
5. The caller sends an email or texts the person to schedule a convenient time for a voice or video phone call. Increasingly, they arrange to talk via an online meeting platform.

> **VOCABULARY**
>
> to **dial** wählen
> to **evolve** sich entwickeln
> **landline** Festnetz
> to **redirect sth** *hier:* etw. verbinden
> **signal strength** Signalstärke
> **switchboard, main line** Zentrale
> to **transfer a call** einen Anruf weiterleiten

   a Hi Amir, is it convenient if I call you about the product design?
   b Let's talk again on Thursday. Let me know when would be a good time.
   c Please wait a moment while I transfer your call.
   d I'm sorry, I didn't catch that. The line is very bad.
   e Good morning Mr Larsson, what can I do for you?

Tell your partner about times you have recently experienced the above situations. Who did you want to speak to and why? What happened next?

6 What are the options if you can't reach someone on the phone? Discuss what you usually do in this case.

7 Listen to three voicemail messages and make a note of the name of each caller, the reason for calling and what action is required.
   08

   Message 1: _____
   Message 2: _____
   Message 3: _____

Listen again and discuss with your partner if and how the messages could be improved. Write your own version of each message and compare in class.

8 Make up a scenario where you fail to reach someone on the phone and decide to leave a voicemail message. Think about the following, based on your personal work situation.

> the reason for the call | the action required | the information the recipient needs

Read the voicemail message to your partner and ask for their feedback.

- Is the message effective?
- Is the message well-structured?
- Have you included all relevant information?
- How would your partner react to getting this message?

ENGLISH FOR TODAY'S WORKPLACE

9 Read some phrases you might hear during a telephone call. Decide whether they are likely to be used at the beginning (B) or the end (E) of the call.

1 Thanks for your help.
2 Please say hello to Moritz.
3 Could I speak to Ms Martinez, please?
4 I don't want to take up any more of your time.
5 Thanks for getting back to me so quickly.
6 Is this a good time to talk?
7 Thanks for calling.
8 Do you have a moment?
9 How can I help you?
10 It's been nice speaking to you.
11 This is Pavel speaking.
12 I'll speak to you again later.

Who could say each of the phrases above – the caller, the recipient or both?

caller: _____   recipient: _____   both: _____

10 Think back to your last few business telephone calls. How did the people on the call say their names – if at all? Compare your answers with a partner.

A I only use my smartphone for work calls so there's no need to say our names. They come up on the display.

B When I call customers, I say my full name even though, in most cases, they can see who's calling.

C In my job, I don't always use a direct line or a mobile number so I introduce myself by name and company.

In Germany, many people answer the telephone by just saying their family name. This sounds a bit abrupt in English! Common ways of giving your name on the phone are to say your full name or just your first name, followed by "speaking".

11 Read Olivia's comment on how she communicates at work. Discuss whether this is also true for you and why/why not.

I talk to people a lot in my job – to my project team, external consultants, and customers. These conversations hardly ever take place as a traditional phone call. First, I send an email or text to figure out a good time to talk. Unless it's a real emergency, I never just pick up the phone. I find it far more efficient to pre-plan a time to talk. When we have agreed on a date and time, I either send a link for an online meeting or make the call – usually video – from my smartphone.

Olivia Callebaut, Antwerp

Match the halves to form complete sentences. Decide which you could use to start a pre-planned telephone call.

1 Would you like me
2 Thank you for
3 I'm sorry that I had to
4 I'm afraid I don't
5 May I ask you to
6 Great to talk

a know Mr Aipoh's extension.
b hold the line?
c to put you through?
d to you again after so long.
e finding the time to talk today.
f contact you at such short notice.

VOCABULARY

extension Durchwahl
to **figure sth out** etw. herausfinden
to **hold the line** am Apparat bleiben
to **pre-plan** vorplanen
to **put so through** jmdn. durchstellen
at short notice kurzfristig

12 The language we use for scheduling a phone call in advance is similar to what we say when making arrangements to meet. Complete the messages to the right with phrases from the box.

> until early evening | how about | have time for | work for | let me just check | shall we say | suit you | particular time | any time after that

13 What can you write to schedule a phone call starting with:
How …? Shall …? Would …? Does …? Are …?
Arrange an appointment to speak to your partner based on your own schedules.

14 It's 10.15 am on Thursday and Jeppe is calling Anna. Listen and mark the correct sentence in each pair.

1. ☐ Anna is surprised that it's already 11.30.
   ☐ Anna doesn't think that it can already be 11.30.
2. ☐ Jeppe is calling to tell Anna he won't be available at 11.30.
   ☐ Jeppe wants to bring forward their call and talk now.
3. ☐ Anna asks Jeppe what he suggests they do now.
   ☐ Anna says she is worried about postponing their talk.
4. ☐ Jeppe is sorry that he doesn't understand what she said.
   ☐ Jeppe appreciates Anna's flexibility.

Think of a time when you had to change an arrangement at short notice. Tell your partner how you contacted the other person and how you explained the situation. What happened next?

Hello Anna, I need to talk to you about the new website design. Do you _____¹ a call later this afternoon?

Hi Jeppe, yes, I know there are some issues with the design, but I have meetings _____² today 😅 _____³ tomorrow or Friday? Would either day _____⁴?

Any _____⁵? I won't be at my desk until 10 tomorrow, but _____ _____⁶ is OK with me if you're available. Friday's a holiday in Denmark! 🇩🇰

_____⁷ Thursday at 11.30? Would that _____⁸ you?

_____⁹ my schedule.

Great!

LANGUAGE FOCUS Easily confused words: already, still, yet

We use *already* to refer to something which happened or may have happened before the moment of speaking. It may mean that the speaker is surprised, especially in a question.
- *Is it **already** 11.30?* (I didn't think it was that late.)

We use *yet* in questions and negatives to talk about things which are expected but haven't happened until now.
- *Is it 11.30 **yet**?* (It must be close to 11.30.)
- *I haven't spoken to Anna **yet**.* (I'm planning to speak to her soon.)

We use *still* to talk about a situation which was true in the past and is the case now too.
- *I **still** need to speak to Anna about the design of the website.*

15 Read some small talk phrases for a video or voice call. Decide which of the phrases you might use. Share any ideas of your own.

a Hi, Phil. How's the weather in San Diego? Better than here, I'm sure!

b I'm so glad we found a time to talk, Juan. You're looking really well, by the way. Have you been on holiday?

c Hello Patrizia. I've had a really wild week here – so much to do, but I suppose you could say the same.

d Good morning Ms Hunter. Thank you very much for finding the time to talk. I hope everything is going well at Sykes Brothers.

How would you respond? Take turns to start the conversations above (change the details to suit your situation) and continue in an appropriate way.

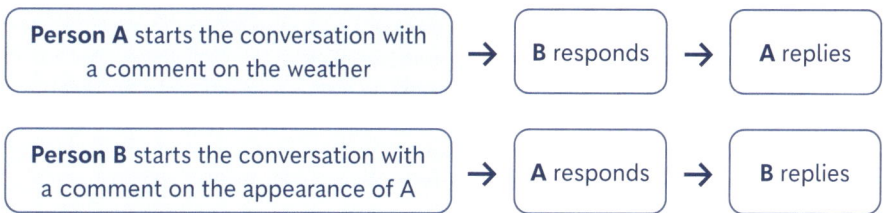

16 You are going to have a phone call with your partner. Follow the instructions and make up any details as you go along.

Partner A is the caller who likes to start with a few minutes of small talk.
Before you make the call, think about what small talk topics you want to talk about and what phrases you can use.

Partner B prefers to get down to business straight away.
Before you answer the call, check the phrases in the Useful Phrases box when you want to move from small talk to business in a friendly and diplomatic way.

USEFUL PHRASES

Transitioning from small talk to business on the phone
- Well, the project is going well, thanks. We're very busy just now so what was it you wanted to speak to me about?
- Listen, (*name of caller*), I'm sorry but I have an online meeting in a few minutes so tell me why …
- Well, that's nice to hear (*after some positive news from the caller*). So, how can I help you?
- I'm glad you've called because I've been meaning to contact you myself. Are you calling about …?
- Anyway, I suppose you're calling about …

17 Most of the language we use on the phone can also be used in other situations. However, there are some phrases which are only used in telephone calls. Decide which phrases are only used on voice or video calls (A) or are used both on and off the phone (B).

1 I'd like to speak to Nico, please.
2 Hold on please, I'll put you through.
3 Is this a good time to talk?
4 Thanks for calling.
5 It's great to see you again.
6 Oh hello, I didn't recognize your voice.
7 It's Maria, again. We were cut off.
8 Dirk isn't here today. Would you like to speak to his assistant?
9 Sorry, I didn't catch that.
10 This is Diego speaking.
11 I'll speak to you again later.
12 The line's not very good, is it? Can you hear me?

18 Read a comment from a time before video calls and texting became commonplace. Is speaking on the telephone still more difficult or stressful than speaking to someone face-to-face despite the option of making a video call? Why do you think so?

> It can be hard to keep a conversation going when you don't see the person you're speaking to with their facial expressions, their body language and their reactions. Telephoning makes me nervous because I'm also afraid I won't understand everything or won't know what to say. Brief silences during a telephone conversation feel a lot more uncomfortable than when speaking face-to-face. People interrupt each a lot more too because they don't see when the other person is getting ready to say something.

Why do many people today prefer texting to telephoning? What are the advantages and disadvantages in a work context?

19 Take turns to read out one "turn" from a telephone call to your partner. The partner responds in any appropriate way as quickly as possible. Write down any suggestions which you particularly like.

- I'd like to speak to Ms Martínez, please.
- Philip isn't in the office today.
- Oh hello, I didn't recognize your voice.
- Is this a good time to talk?
- She's in a meeting now.
- I think she'll be available after lunch.
- I'm returning your call.

10 Compare your responses in class and discuss if they are all appropriate. Then listen to the exchanges to hear if your ideas were similar to the originals. Note down any phrases that you would like to use yourself in work calls.

20 Based on the situation in the partner files, role play a telephone call. Check you understand and know how to use the Useful Phrases below before you look at your file.

▷ Partner Files, File 2: Partner A, page 68 | Partner B, page 71

USEFUL PHRASES   Difficult phone calls

Technical problems
- It's a very bad line.
- My battery's low.
- Does your battery need charging?
- Hello? You're breaking up.
- I couldn't get a signal.
- We were cut off.

Checking understanding
- So, you're saying …
- Can I just check that I understood that correctly?
- Let me see if I got that right.

Problems understanding
- I'm sorry, I didn't catch that.
- Could you speak up a bit, please?
- Would you mind slowing down a bit?
- Could you repeat the name of …?
- Could you explain that in a different way?
- I'm sorry, but I can't follow you.

- So, to confirm …
- If I've understood you correctly, …
- Did you say first or third?

ENGLISH FOR TODAY'S WORKPLACE

21 Read this comment on good practice in business communication. What makes spoken language (any language) easier to understand?

BBC   Best Business Communication

Topics
AI
Branding
Customer journeys
Email
Plain language
Speaking skills

▶ see all topics

Excellent spoken and written communication skills benefit customers and organizations. There seems to be a mistaken idea that long sentences with complex words, spoken quickly make the speaker sound smart and professional. If it sounds complex, it must be good. In fact, the result is a lack of intelligibility and credibility.

The primary goal of communication is to pass on information so that readers or listeners understand the message quickly and correctly. Nobody has ever complained that someone was too easy to understand!

Contact us for information on our training events

VOCABULARY

credibility Glaubwürdigkeit
intelligibility Verständlichkeit
mistaken irrtümlich
smart *hier:* intelligent

22 Have you ever experienced a communication breakdown with a business contact which was a result of language difficulties? Share the details with your partner and talk about why this happened and how you dealt with the problem.

23 We change the meaning of a sentence by stressing different words. Doing this clearly is a good strategy for getting your message across. Match sentences (1-5) with the correct interpretation (a-e). The stressed word is underlined

1 I could <u>do</u> this for you.
2 <u>I</u> could do this for you.
3 I could do <u>this</u> for you.
4 I could do this for <u>you</u>.
5 I <u>could</u> do this for you.

a It may be difficult and perhaps not a good idea.
b I can't offer you anything else.
c I agree to your request.
d Don't expect anyone else to do it.
e Not everyone gets this offer.

24 Find the pairs of phrases which have the same meaning. Compare your answers with a partner.

get hold of | breaking up | return a call | keep in contact | reach | ring off | the phone signal is poor | lose contact | give someone a buzz | cut off | call back | stay in touch | call someone | end the conversation

*Although it may sound simpler, **informal language** may be more difficult to understand than standard phrases. Adapt your language according to the language level of the person you're speaking to.*

25 How do you usually finish business telephone calls? Make a note of a few phrases you use (in German or English) or what the people you talk to say, and compare them with your partner's phrases.

26 In order not to end a call too abruptly, it's a good idea to use a three-step process. Match phrases a–i with the corresponding steps.

a Have a good day. Bye now.
b I'll look forward to your email.
c Thanks again and until next time.
d Well, I have a meeting very shortly.
e I'll send you the information tomorrow so you can let me know what you think.
f So, don't let me take up any more of your time.
g We'll talk again soon. Take care.
h I'll have the samples sent to you right away.
i OK, it's been great talking to you.

Step 1: Signal you want to end the call: ☐ ☐ ☐
Step 2: Review what you decided: ☐ ☐ ☐
Step 3: Sign off: ☐ ☐ ☐

> *Signalling* that you are ready to end the call often starts with words like "well", "so", "okay". This shows you want to change the subject.

27 In pairs, discuss how to complete this telephone conversation in the most suitable way. Listen to compare your version with the call. If your answers are different, double-check that they also fit into the phrase grammatically.

Lydia: Lydia Anderson _____ ¹. Hello Mr Hansen. Thank you for calling back at such _____ ². _____ ³ in Munich now? Pretty cold, I expect.

Fritz: Hello Ms Anderson. Actually, I'm in Vienna today – and yes, it's pretty cold here, too! Anyway, I don't want to _____ ⁴ of your time. I understand you want to find out more about the latest model of our civilian drones.

Lydia: Yes, that's right. What's different about the new drone?

Fritz: Well, they can get much …

Lydia: Hello? You're _____ ⁵. Mr Hansen, are you still there?

Fritz: Yes, I'm sorry. The signal _____ ⁶ at the moment.

Lydia: I'm afraid I _____ ⁷ the last thing you said.

Fritz: Well, I was saying they can get much closer to buildings and the camera quality is far better. The live images are really excellent. You know, I'd like to _____ ⁸. I'm in the UK in two weeks – why don't I come to Manchester so we can talk in more detail?

Lydia: Brilliant! Let me _____ ⁹. Would Tuesday, the 7th of November _____ ¹⁰ for you?

Fritz: That sounds like an ex …

> Notice the different structure of phrases with the same meaning:
> • Would that be / Is that convenient for you?
> • Would / Does that suit you?
> • Would / Does that work for you?

ENGLISH FOR TODAY'S WORKPLACE

OVER TO YOU

 1 Read a comment about communication channels for sales staff. Discuss how this compares with the way you communicate in your role at work and what you have to consider.

> With digital communication constantly evolving, it's difficult to decide the best way to communicate with customers. Some people don't want to be disturbed by phone calls, others get annoyed at too many emails, but both have their place in our industry.
>
> Apart from being a more personal way to communicate, customers recognize that making a phone call means more time and effort on the part of the sales staff and appreciate that. During a phone call, the caller has the attention of the customer. They might just delete an email without even reading it.
>
>
>
> The benefit of sending emails is that it saves time. In addition, sales staff can reach a far greater number of people easily. Personalizing an email doesn't take long. The recipients can deal with an email in their own time so may react more positively in the end.
>
> The answer is to find the correct balance and include instant messaging for short updates when appropriate.

2 Referring back to the bar chart you completed on page 18 and your discussion in exercise 1, choose one of these options.

Option 1: Write a profile of an interaction you had recently in your job which included an important telephone call. Mention any other forms of communication (email, text, online meeting, F2F) as appropriate.

Option 2: Write a profile of a typical interaction you might have at work which includes making important telephone calls. Mention any other forms of communication (email, text, online meeting, F2F) as appropriate.

 3 SIMULATION

1 Work with a partner to simulate a phone call. Take turns to base this on the profile of the interaction each partner created in exercise 2 (option 1 or 2).
- Together, go through the details of the interaction, asking and answering any questions which may arise to make sure the situation is clear to both of you.
- Look back through the unit to review telephoning phrases which may be useful.
- Focus on the telephone call only. Partner A explains the reason for calling and describes the course of the call. Partner B asks for clarification if necessary.
- Simulate the call with Partner A playing their own role. If the conversation develops in a different way from the original, just go with the flow and improvise!
- Repeat the procedure with Partner B's profile.

2 **Debriefing**
- Did the telephone calls reflect realistic situations for you?
- Did you use telephone phrases appropriately?
- Did you manage to improvise and continue the conversations successfully?

THIS UNIT LOOKS AT …

- everyday workplace interactions: describing, explaining, expressing opinions
- showing people around the company
- presenting and explaining company policy

4 All in a day's work

Look at the topics in the word cloud and discuss which are having the biggest impact on how we work today.

Complete the statements below with a word or phrase from the word cloud. Do you agree with the comments?

> corporate language policies   hybrid working   back-to-the-office   flexible working hours
> diverse workforce   **Workplaces Today**   forced fun   barrier-free access
> teamwork skills   workspace design   four-day week   paper-light office   carbon footprint

1 Although _____ has become the "new normal" for the majority of employees, as far as I know, many companies are working on a _____ strategy.

2 Different ways of working lead to big changes in _____, but as a wheelchair user, it seems to me that there is still some work to be done to optimize _____.

3 Some companies are piloting a _____, but I can't imagine that working well.

4 Having a lot of staff with _____ working from home with little in-person contact make _____ more challenging but even more crucial.

5 A lot of companies have reduced their budget for social events and, if you ask me, a lot of people are relieved because they didn't enjoy what we used to call the _____!

6 One result of having an increasingly _____ has been the need to change _____. In our case, this means that our working language is now English.

7 Businesses know that it's important to reduce their _____ – if only to boost their reputation. Becoming a _____ by replacing paper-based processes with digitized documents as far as possible is a good place to start.

ENGLISH FOR TODAY'S WORKPLACE

VOCABULARY

barrier-free access Barrierefreiheit
to boost sth etw. verstärken, verbessern
carbon footprint CO2-Fußabdruck
challenging schwierig, herausfordernd
crucial von entscheidender Bedeutung
digitized digitalisiert
forced fun erzwungener Spaß
relieved erleichtert

 1 In pairs, discuss at least three of the topics from the word cloud on page 38. Use the questions and Useful Phrases below to help you express your opinions.

1 How challenging is it for companies to implement and why?
2 How important will this be in the future and why?
3 What is the situation in your own company?

Share your conclusions in class.

USEFUL PHRASES   Expressing opinions

Giving your opinion
- As far as I know, …
- It seems to me that …
- It's important to note that …
- Well, if you ask me, I think …
- I can't imagine how …
- One thing that I've noticed is …

Expressing doubt / disagreement
- You have a point, but …
- Yes, but don't you think that …
- I see what you mean, but …
- I'm sorry, but I don't agree with you on that.

Showing agreement
- Absolutely.
- Exactly.
- That's true.
- That's just what I was thinking.

Watch out!
*to **notice** = merken, wahrnehmen*
*a **notice** = ein Schild, Aushang*

*to **make a note of sth** = etw. notieren, aufschreiben*
*a **note** = eine Notiz*
*to **note that** … = zur Kenntnis nehmen*

 2 Read some comments on corporate language policies.
From this starting point, make a list of arguments for and against making English the working language of a company in Germany.

A Like it or not, English is the language of global business so companies can improve their efficiency by enforcing English as their working language.

B I work for a start-up in Berlin. When we hire new people, their technical skills are more important to us than whether they can speak German. Our office is totally multi-lingual, but everyone speaks English.

C There are risks with an English-only policy because staff with strong language skills are not always the ones with the highest levels of job-related competence.

Report your conclusions to the class by completing these sentences.

1 Our strongest arguments for making English the working language are …
2 As far as arguments against are concerned, we think …
3 In order to implement a policy like this, companies have to …
4 So, the conclusion we've come to is that …

UNIT 4: ALL IN A DAY'S WORK

3 Read a definition of onboarding. Discuss how the process of onboarding new employees may have changed in recent years because of changes in the workplace.

Onboarding is the process of …

- integrating new hires into an organization by enabling them to acquire the knowledge, skills, behaviours and values needed to work effectively and become "insiders".
- familiarizing new customers and clients with a company's processes, products and services.

VOCABULARY

to **acquire sth** etw. erwerben, erlangen
behaviours Verhaltensweisen, Auftreten
to **familiarize so with sth** jmdn. mit etw. vertraut machen
new hires neu eingestellte Mitarbeiter*innen
values (pl.) Werte

4 At the beginning of the onboarding process, new hires need to get to know the business premises and meet their co-workers. Use the expressions in the Useful Phrases box to explain where these places are in your department or building.

bicycle parking garage | car park | CEO's office | conference room | first aid room | hot-desking space | kitchen | meeting room | post room | server room | wheelchair ramps | your own office

UK, Ireland, India, Australia, South Africa, Mexico:
ground floor, first floor

North America, China, Japan, South Korea:
first floor, second floor

USEFUL PHRASES Describing locations

- The stairs are **next to / near** the lift.
  The restrooms are **nearby**.
- The break room is **opposite** the lift, **between** the kitchen **and** the office supplies room.
- The conference room is **on the top floor.** There's a fire extinguisher **in the corridor outside.**
- The server room is **in the basement**.
- There's a coffee vending machine **on the right-hand side of** the reception area.
  The fire escape is **on the left** of the staircase.
- The restrooms are **behind** those glass doors, **in front of** the entrance to the canteen.

 With your partner, talk about the location of any other places in your company building.

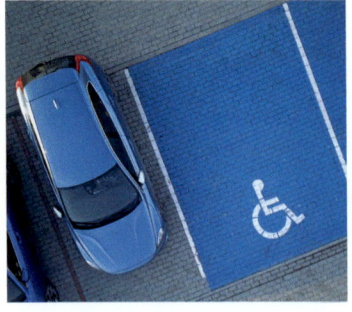

ENGLISH FOR TODAY'S WORKPLACE

5 Add the places to the photos.

hot-desking bench | silent pod | meeting booth | soft-seating area | quiet zone | informal meeting area

a _____

b _____

c _____

d _____

e _____

f _____

Discuss why we might need places like these in a modern office and whether your company has them. Take the following questions into consideration.

1 If so, how often and for what reasons do you use these places?
2 If not, how would they improve your working environment?

6 Antonia is showing Dominic, her new co-worker, around the company building. Listen to their conversation and mark the places above (a–f) which she shows him.

Listen again and complete the phrases you hear.

1 Well, _____ the building.
2 So, take _____ – it's changed so much.
3 We're changing our office space to optimize the design _____.
4 We've _____ because there are never more than 50% of staff on-site.
5 If you _____, you'll see one of the hot-desking benches.
6 We have at least one area like that _____.
7 Here and _____.
8 We have silent pods – the ones that look like telephone booths – _____ alone.
9 There are also a few booths there, _____ talk.
10 Then we can _____ the quiet zone.

Which of the sentences above does Antonia use …

a … to show him around? _____
b … to explain the reasons for the new workspace design? _____

7 Tell your partner what you remember about the onboarding process when you joined your present company.

8 Read what Dominic says and match the excerpts (a–f) with the stages of his onboarding process.

"The onboarding process for my job as a software engineering consultant lasts for six weeks. My company outsources the paperwork to an external HR service provider so submitting documents all happened online, but I can email the company if I have a query. ▇
I work remotely most of the time, but, following the instructions in the company employee manual, on my first day I went to the head office to pick up my ID/access badge, my company smartphone and find out how to order my company laptop. ▇
Antonia showed me around the building. It seems the workspaces have been totally redesigned to fit in with the hybrid working style of most staff members. It was nice to meet a few of the colleagues who were there that day when we had lunch in the canteen. ▇
Being there also gave me the chance to meet the other new hires. Our manager explained that all our onboarding training was self-led online and that all of us get a separate time slot every Friday to present what we've learned that week. ▇ These sessions are open to anybody in the company who's interested. This is extremely challenging because the presentation is always followed by a Q&A session. ▇
The company assigns a mentor to each new hire. ▇ Luckily for me, my mentor has turned out to be Devika Kumar, who I already know from when we worked together in Frankfurt a few years back. She's the person I can contact if I have any questions during or after the onboarding process."

a "So how long have you been working here?"
"I joined the company about six months ago. It's a nice change from my previous job."

b "This week I've been working on architectural design so today I'd like to talk about customizing our software for the client's system."

c "Darf ich meine Frage auf Deutsch stellen? Ich bin kein Software-Ingenieur, deshalb möchte ich wissen, wie Sie einem Kunden die Änderungen an den Firewall-Regeln erklären würden."

d "I'm working on my presentation for Friday and I'd like to check how we track business transactions from the java application. So, if you have a moment …"

e I have a query about translating my documents. Do you require certified translations or can I ask a bi-lingual friend to translate them for me?

f Bitte holen Sie Ihren digitalen Firmenausweis an Ihrem ersten Arbeitstag in Raum 208 ab.

Explain your answers to your partner.

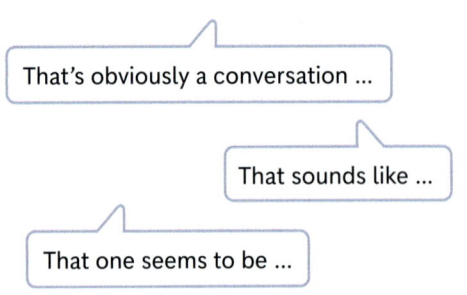

That's obviously a conversation …

That sounds like …

That one seems to be …

> **Watch out!**
> The manager asked **all of us** (NOT: ~~everybody of us~~) to give a presentation on Friday.
> Devika and I **met** when we were both working in Frankfurt. (NOT: ~~we met us when~~)
> **Anybody**, but not **everybody** can ask a question.
> **anybody** = an individual member of a group; it doesn't matter which person
> **everybody** = all the members of a group

Share your opinion of the onboarding process Dominic describes with your partner. How does it compare with your own experience?

ENGLISH FOR TODAY'S WORKPLACE

9 Listen to Max explaining his company's smartphone policy. Number the signposting phrases (a-f) in the order you hear them (1-6).

a One very important issue for us is …
b So how does this work, …
c The topic I'd like to talk about today is …
d That's the reason why …
e The starting point is that …
f I'd also like to mention …

> *Signposting language* refers to the words and phrases used to guide listeners through a presentation or an explanation so they can follow an argument and understand the relationship between the points.

10 Max is easy to follow because, apart from signposting clearly, he pauses effectively to get his message across. Listen to Max again and focus on how he speaks rather than what he says.

11 Now try reading these examples out loud to notice the difference when you speak yourself.

Example 1

It doesn't really matter if people speak with a strong accent as long as they can be understood easily.
However, it's important that people make sure they're speaking slowly and clearly if they have an accent, isn't it?

Example 2 / = short pause, // = longer pause

It doesn't really matter / if people speak with a strong accent / as long as they can be understood easily. //
However / it's important / that people make sure they're speaking slowly and clearly / if they have an accent // isn't it?//

 12 MEDIATION

Imagine that your partner doesn't speak German and you have to explain one aspect of company policy to them in English.

1 Follow the instructions in the files.
  Partner Files, File 3: Partner A, page 68 | Partner B, page 71
2 Check the vocabulary list for your topic before you start to plan your talk.
3 Remember to use signposting language and pauses effectively.
4 Take turns to mediate the information. Before you listen, check your partner's vocabulary list.
5 With your partner, discuss how often and for what reasons you have to switch between English and German in your job.

VOCABULARY (Partner A)

to **aim to do sth** etw. anstreben
to **come into force** in Kraft treten
to **commute** pendeln
consumption Verbrauch
to **promote sth** *hier:* etw. fördern
to **implement sth** etw. umsetzen
sustainable nachhaltig

VOCABULARY (Partner B)

a choice of eine Auswahl an
collaborative work gemeinschaftliches Arbeiten
to **feel connected to sth** sich etw. verbunden fühlen
key point Eckpunkt
personal communication direkter Austausch
to **redesign sth** etw. umgestalten
to **take sth into account** etw. berücksichtigen

UNIT 4: ALL IN A DAY'S WORK

13 Read some comments about factory tours and discuss your own experience – as host or visitor.

A I took a delegation from our branch office near Bucharest on a tour of the new factory.

B We were shown around the production plant in Anting before heading back to Shanghai for the meeting.

C Although we knew each other from online meetings, the first time I met our Indian supplier in person was when I showed him around our smart warehouse.

D I gave the company tour in English because it was the only language all of the visitors spoke.

E All new hires were taken around the shop floor to give them insight into our manufacturing processes.

F The tour was interesting but the best part was when we were offered refreshments at the end!

> **VOCABULARY**
>
> **branch office** Zweigstelle
> to **head back** zurückfahren, zurückgehen
> **plant** *hier:* Fabrik, Werk
> **shop floor** Fertigung

14 Look at the verbs in exercise 13 again. Write them in the correct column in the table.

Active verbs (what the host did)	**Passive verbs** (what happened to the visitors)

15 A tour of the company is often on the agenda for visitors. Who are the most common visitors to your company? What do they want to see? Discuss these questions with your partner.

> business partners | colleagues from foreign subsidiaries | customers | general public | inspectors | investors | the media | suppliers | visitors from head office

What are the main differences between taking an individual or a group on a tour of the company?

ENGLISH FOR TODAY'S WORKPLACE

16 Match the sentence halves to find ways of signalling to a group that you are ready to start a company visit.

1	If you're ready,	a	take your coats.
2	By the way, if anyone would like to freshen up	b	where our in-house innovation starts.
3	The visit will take about 90 minutes	c	I'll say a few words about our product portfolio.
4	Our first stop today is the main R&D lab,	d	to ask questions at any time.
5	My colleagues will	e	before we start, the restrooms are on the right.
6	While we're walking over there,	f	there's a lot to see.
7	We should get going now because	g	we can head over to the factory.
8	By the way, please feel free	h	so we don't want to waste any time.

Rearrange the sentences into what you consider the most logical order as in the example.

5/a

17 A European delegation is visiting a Chinese company which manufactures parts for the automotive industry. Listen to some excerpts from their company tour and underline the seven phrases in the Useful Phrases box that you hear. Read through the phrases before you listen.

> **USEFUL PHRASES**   Giving company tours
>
> **Guiding visitors**
> - Please follow me down the stairs to the production area.
> - Please keep together at all times.
> - Before we go in, please put on this protective clothing.
> - So now, let's go into the lab.
> - Do you have any questions before we move on?
> - If everyone has had the chance to see everything here, shall we head over to the shop floor?
>
> **Questions to ask**
> - You mentioned earlier that this line has the most downtime, right?
> - Are you planning to phase out the equipment?
> - How long does it take to retool the line when you switch to the new technology?
>
> **Pointing things out**
> - So, this is where we manufacture parts for trucks.
> - Just over on the left, you can see the entrance to our R&D lab.
> - I'd like to draw your attention to our new production line for electric vehicles. It's really state-of-the-art.
> - Behind that door is the control room.
> - The quality control department is beyond the second production hall.
> - Coming up now is something which I know will interest you all.
>
> **Finishing the tour**
> - Well, that brings us to the end of the tour for today.
> - I hope I've been able to give you some insight into our manufacturing processes.
> - Let's make our way back to the conference room. I'm sure that some refreshments are waiting for us!

18 Listen again and complete the sentences.

1 We don't want to _____ anybody.
2 Feel _____ to ask.
3 The equipment is no longer _____ to be quite honest with you.
4 We're _____ it very shortly.
5 How long _____ to retool the line?
6 We should _____ to the quality control department.

UNIT 4: ALL IN A DAY'S WORK

19 Find the two most important reasons for hosting each kind of company meeting. What other reasons could there be?

1 all-hands meeting
2 away day
3 company social event
4 town hall

a Part of onboarding process for new hires.
b Announcing new hires and departures.
c Presenting and discussing the vision and long-term goals of the company.
d Creating more cohesive, high-performing teams.
e Allowing employees to engage with the leadership in a two-way conversation.
f Informing about a visiting delegation from abroad.
g Offering a fun event to motivate staff.
h Encouraging staff to feel connected to the company.

> Typically, an **all-hands meeting** takes place regularly for updates and changes. A **town hall** focuses on open discussion and takes place less often. Both are large-scale meetings.

Exchange opinions with your partner on whether companies in general and your company in particular organize fewer or more of any of these events, spending less or more money on them than in the past. Share your opinions in class.

> **LANGUAGE FOCUS**   Fewer and less
>
> It's easy to confuse "fewer" and "less" because both are the opposite of "more". One way of avoiding mistakes is to remember that "fewer" = *not as many* and "less" = *not as much*.
> We use "fewer" for **countable nouns** and "less" for **uncountable nouns**.
>
> *This week I had fewer meetings than last week, but this didn't mean that I had less work to do.*

 20 Read the quote from an event planner and discuss how to plan inclusive corporate events. Check the Useful Phrases box to help you present your ideas in a convincing way.

"Social events are a great idea to promote a cohesive workforce, but there are a lot of pitfalls when your staff is very diverse. And a diverse workforce is the norm today, right? Not everyone in the company will be attracted by the same type of event and some great ideas will be inaccessible for others. Issues to take into account are interests, dietary requirements, barrier-free access, cultural background, family situation. This is a long list so where to start?"

> **USEFUL PHRASES**   Presenting a convincing argument in four steps
>
> **Step 1: Expressing an opinion**
> To me, a helpful first step for us would be to ask staff for their suggestions.
> **Step 2: Providing a supporting argument**
> What's more, that would signal that we value their input.
> **Step 3: Reformulating**
> So, in other words, this would be a way of including staff in the planning process.
> **Step 4: Summarizing**
> All things considered, this would be the best way to avoid wasting time with unworkable ideas.

21 Think about a situation when you have had to make a suggestion in your job (e.g. choosing a new supplier, hiring a new team-member, etc.). Present your argument to your partner.

ENGLISH FOR TODAY'S WORKPLACE

OVER TO YOU

 1 Read two items of business news about the present state of business travel. Share your opinion on the topic with your partner by answering the questions below.

(Not) back to normal?
The days of big-spending business travel may be over for good. Research suggests that fewer big-spenders are splashing out on first-class tickets and luxury hotels. In general, fewer people are travelling on business, and those who do are travelling less often. Company travel budgets have shrunk noticeably.

Should companies go the extra mile?
Business travellers are ready for take-off again. One reason is that they fear business relations are in danger if business partners don't meet in person any more. However, employees today expect quality, flexibility and safety from their companies. They want to have a say in their own travel arrangements.

1 Why do people travel on business? Think of as many reasons as you can.
2 What factors have had an effect on business travel since the 2000s?
3 From the point of view of an employer, do you think it's worth spending a lot of money on business travel?
4 Have you been personally affected by any changes in your company's business travel policy? If so, how?

> **VOCABULARY**
>
> to **go back to normal** zur Normalität zurückkehren
> to **go the extra mile** sich ins Zeug legen
> to **have a say in sth** bei etw. Mitspracherecht haben
> to **shrink** schrumpfen
> to **splash out on sth** für etw. tief in die Tasche greifen

Watch out!
- *Concern about their carbon footprint* **has had an effect** *on the level of business travel a company allows.*
- *The pandemic* **affected** *the way we think about business travel by showing that online meetings with overseas business partners can be just as* **effective**.

 2 SIMULATION ─────────────────

Showing a visitor around your company.

1 In pairs, plan the scenario, making it as realistic as you can for the situation in your company.
   - Who is the visitor? Where do they come from?
   - What is the purpose of the visit?
   - What part of the company will you visit – the office building, factory, labs, warehouse, etc.?
   - What technical/specialized vocabulary will you need?

2 Decide on roles – one of you is yourself, the other is the visitor.

3 Look back through the unit to refresh your memory of suitable language for each role. Read through the transcript to audio 12 on page 78.

4 Keeping these steps in mind, simulate the situation.
   greetings → small talk → starting the tour → moving from one place to another → explaining, asking and answering questions → ending the tour

5 Debriefing
   - Was the visit informative?
   - Did the tour run smoothly?
   - Did you both react appropriately to what the other person said?

UNIT 4: ALL IN A DAY'S WORK

THIS UNIT LOOKS AT …

- virtual and face-to-face interaction and collaboration
- meetings: facilitation and participation
- conversation management

5 Working together

 Discuss whether the results from the following snap survey reflect your experience.

Data shows that employees spend an ever-increasing number of their working hours in meetings so we decided to carry out a snap survey among our own employees. This is what we found:

1. Meetings take up at least 30% of my working hours.
2. Too often, meetings take me away from my "real work".
3. I regularly feel overwhelmed by the amount of time I spend taking part in meetings.
4. We waste too much time on synchronous communication. A lot of information-sharing could be done by email.
5. At least 20% of the meetings which take place in the company are poorly organized.
6. Agile methodology depends on frequent short meetings. This way of working has increased the time I spend in meetings.

VOCABULARY

to **carry out sth** etw. durchführen
snap survey Kurzumfrage
to **take part in sth** an etw. teilnehmen
to **take place** stattfinden
to **take so away from sth** jmdn. von etw. abhalten
to **take up (time)** (Zeit) in Anspruch nehmen
overwhelmed *hier:* überlastet

 Discuss how to make meetings an effective use of everyone's time to optimize outcomes. Share your opinions in class.

 1 **An internet search for rules on effective meetings presented these suggestions:**

a the 40-20-40 rule
b the 10-10-10 rule
c the rule of 7
d the 5 second rule

Idiomatic expressions: Guessing the right answer
We were spot on! = completely correct
We were miles out! = completely wrong
We were quite close. = more or less correct

In pairs, first discuss what you think the numbers refer to. Afterwards, check the answers in the files.
Partner Files, File 4: Partner A, page 69 | Partner B, page 72

ENGLISH FOR TODAY'S WORKPLACE

2 What types of meetings have you taken part in recently? Tell your partner the purpose of these meetings and describe your role.

> The term *jour fixe* is not unknown in Europe when using English as a lingua franca, but it is more common to refer to "regular meetings" in English-speaking countries.

all hands | brainstorming | debriefing | in-person | kick-off | offboarding | onboarding | one-on-one | online | regular | retrospective | stand-up | status update | working

3 Before you listen to some short excerpts from meetings, complete each sentence with one suitable word. Compare your answers with a partner, then listen to check.

15

1 Let's get _____, shall we? We need to _____ up with some new ideas on how we can improve sales.

2 Pedro, I can't see you. Can you _____ on your video, please?

3 As this is our first meeting, shall we start by everyone introducing their _____ in the project?

4 OK, so we've identified a few things we could have done _____. Anything else before we _____ on?

What happened next? Match the excerpts (1–4) above with the most suitable follow-on sentence (a–d).

   a Thanks. Now, to everyone – when you're not speaking, please remember to mute your mic.
   b Right, so that leads me to my next question – what are we going to do differently next time?
   c Any and all ideas are welcome at this point.
   d So let me go first. Part of my role will be liaising with everyone about major aspects of the project.

Where would you expect to hear the excerpts (1–4)? Match each one to a meeting type. In pairs, choose one and continue the meeting as you think it could develop.

an online meeting   a kick-off meeting   a debriefing   a brainstorming meeting

4 In pairs, read a comment about multi-tasking in meetings and share your views.

"Everyone thinks they're good at multitasking. They feel more productive when they multi-task during a meeting. It's a golden opportunity to listen to project updates while answering urgent emails – some may not even be work-related … Seems to be a win-win situation, but studies have shown that most people are not nearly as good at multi-tasking as they think they are."

Look at the word cloud and compare your multi-tasking preferences in class. Which three activities are the most popular?

playing online games | writing work-related emails | checking your work calendar | texting with a friend | browsing social media | **What people do during meetings** | catching up with urgent work | reading the news | drawing/doodling | online shopping

UNIT 5: WORKING TOGETHER | 49

5 Rank these behaviours according to how often you encounter them in meetings and how disruptive they are. When attendees …

are obviously not listening carefully | arrive late | dominate the discussion | don't contribute | don't show up | have side conversations | seem to be multi-tasking

In pairs, explain your opinion by completing the following sentences as appropriate.

1 To me, the very worst thing is when …
2 It can be very frustrating when attendees …
3 When someone …, it holds up the meeting.
4 At our meetings, attendees tend not to …
5 One thing I don't encounter often is that …
6 To be honest, it doesn't worry me if …

6 Read about and discuss the pros and cons of different meeting cultures. How would you characterize your own company's meeting culture?

> Our meetings start with chit chat, have a loose structure and a flexible agenda. They often overrun. The next steps are not always clearly formulated, but we have a high level of trust and collaboration.

> Our meetings are very results-driven with clear goals, a detailed agenda and strict timekeeping. We don't spend time on informal conversations during meetings, but leave that for chats in the breakroom.

> No one spends more than four hours a week sitting in a meeting. In addition, we have regular stand-ups and even spontaneous walking meetings. If another form of communication is more effective, we choose that rather than calling a meeting.

*Not everyone likes the tone of **ground rules** when talking about team collaboration. Consider using other terms like **guidelines, meeting code of conduct** or **meeting norms**.*

 7 MEDIATION

Imagine you have been given the task of making an English version of your company's meeting ground rules for co-workers who don't speak German.

1 Look at a copy of your company's or project team's meeting guidelines in German or write a list of the rules you personally would like to see. Alternatively, use the rules on page 86.
2 Now write a version in English using as many of the words in the Vocabulary box as you can.
3 Use an app to translate the original German version of the guidelines. Compare the translation with your own set of rules in English. Make any adjustments you like.
4 Share your final version in class and discuss the best way to formulate the rules.

VOCABULARY

agenda item Tagesordnungspunkt
to **allocate roles** Rollen verteilen
to **allow for sth** *hier:* etw. einplanen
to **contribute to sth** *hier:* sich in etw. einbringen
to **determine sth** etw. festlegen
to **ensure sth** *hier:* für etw. sorgen
goal-oriented zielgerichtet
to **hear so out** jmdn. ausreden lassen
leeway Zeitpuffer
to **make sth available** etw. bereitstellen
to **mute a mic** Mikrofon stummschalten
to **stick to sth** bei etw. bleiben
to **overrun (time)** überziehen

8 Read the Useful Phrases and discuss in what situation the facilitator might use each one.

> **USEFUL PHRASES** Telling people what is expected tactfully and professionally
>
> - I'd like to start by reminding everyone of our meeting guidelines.
> - Let's aim to finish the meeting on time by avoiding distractions.
> - Please don't forget to click on the raise hand button if you want to contribute.
> - We appreciate your input, Jaime. Thanks. Now, let's hear from the others. Tom?
> - Assuming that everyone has read the agenda, let's start with our first item.
> - Let's come back to this next time when Gillian can explain what she meant.
> - I don't think I need to tell you how important it is to stay on topic.
> - As you can see, our client has given us a very tight schedule.

> **VOCABULARY**
>
> to **contribute to sth** *hier*: zur Diskussion beitragen
> **distraction** Ablenkung
> **tight schedule** straffer Zeitplan

9 Imagine you are moderating the next project meeting in English and want to refer to the guidelines you created in exercise 7 in a professional and tactful way. What can you say? Share your ideas with a partner.

10 There are situations during a meeting when the facilitator has to intervene. Match the correct category (1–4) with the phrases (a–d).

1 transitioning to the next point on the agenda
2 handling an interruption
3 keeping the meeting on track
4 asking for input

a That's an interesting point but not our topic today so I'll make a note of it for next week's meeting.
b I'm sorry, Katja, but I'll have to stop you there, we have to move on.
c This would be a good time to share any suggestions you have.
d Stefano has already raised his hand so let's hear from him first, please.

In pairs, come up with at least two more phrases you could use in each category.

11 In a well-planned and well-run meeting, a good facilitator keeps everyone focused by asking for comments and checking understanding. Complete the phrases below with words from the box.

concerns | hear | make | mind | position | with

1 Does that _____ sense to you, Amir?
2 Is this your _____, David?
3 I'd like to _____ from you, Xue.
4 Do you have any other _____, Leena?
5 Is there anything on your _____, Anny?
6 Are you all _____ me?

Which of the questions or statements mean the following?

Tell us what you are worried about.
Did I make myself clear?
Tell us your opinion.

UNIT 5: WORKING TOGETHER

12 Find pairs of verbs which have the same meaning when talking about meetings. In one case, there are four verbs with the same meaning. Check the words in a dictionary if necessary.

| attend | chair | circulate | compile | draw up | facilitate | hold | host | join | log in to | moderate | run | send round | solve | sort out | take part in |

Take turns to use verbs from the box to tell your partner about your recent meetings.

"At the last meeting I chaired, the attendees complained that I hadn't circulated the relevant data in time."

"Ellen drew up a list of meeting guidelines. Number one was to be sure to log in on time!"

13 Look at some tasks involved in planning and running a meeting. Match the tasks (1–6) with what the facilitator might say (a–l) by writing the letters in the boxes.

1 Establishing the ground rules
2 Explaining timing of meeting
3 Building rapport
4 Outlining meeting objectives/outcomes
5 Encouraging participation
6 Communicating action points

a Let's have a quick update from everyone on what they've been doing.
b Our goal today is to identify the obstacles to delivering the project on time.
c We need input from the software developers, so that's your task, Marcus.
d Can I ask everyone to share their concerns about the project?
e OK, that's agreed. Alyssa will contact our suppliers immediately.
f We need to be 100% ready to report to the board by Friday.
g If you want to contribute, please use the raise hand button.
h We should aim to finish on time.
i Thank you all for logging in on time. How are you all?
j I'd like to hear from each of you on this.
k Activate the mute button, when you're not speaking.
l We've scheduled this meeting to last 50 minutes.

> **Watch out!**
> In time = before it's too late
> On time = punctually, at the agreed time

With a partner, think of what else you could say to deal with tasks 1–6. Then compare your ideas with another pair. Which of the tasks do you feel most confident about dealing with in English?

14 Think about a meeting you took part in recently and make notes under these headings.

Type of meeting	My role	What went well	What went less well	Lessons learned

Share your thoughts in a group.

15 Share your experience of stand-up meetings with your partner. What are the main benefits of this format?

> A **(daily) stand-up** or **scrum** refers to any short meeting which is called to give updates or make a quick decision.

52   ENGLISH FOR TODAY'S WORKPLACE

Listen to part of a stand-up meeting and answer the questions. Jessica is the scrum master.

1 Why doesn't Jessica wait for Maxim to join the meeting?
2 What positive news does Rohan have for the team?
3 Rohan talks about "takeaways", "bringing the team up to speed" and "more problems down the line". What do these expressions mean?
4 What obstacle is Rohan facing?
5 Does Marta mention the same problem as Rohan?
6 Why does Jessica interrupt Marta?

Daily scrum agenda:
What did you accomplish yesterday?
What are you working on today?
What obstacles are you facing?

16 Match some of the verbs you heard with their meanings in the context of the meeting. Listen again to check.

1 to block so or sth
2 to double-check sth
3 to hang around
4 to hold so or sth up
5 to reach out to so
6 to sidebar sth

a to stay in a place or stay online
b to make contact
c to delay dealing with an issue
d to look at something again
e to prevent work from going ahead
f to create a delay

Read the Transcript on page 79 (Track 16) and make a note of the phrases you can use in your meetings.

 17 SIMULATION

Imagine you are taking part in a stand-up with your partner to report on the present status of your work.

*Make what you say more listener-friendly by breaking up your sentences into small, understandable **chunks** (usually a few words) and **pausing** after each chunk.*

1 **Choose one option:**
   • Base your status update on the three questions in the daily scrum agenda.
   • Widen the scope and consider these questions: What have you accomplished recently? What are you working on at present? What obstacles are you facing?

2 **Think about and make notes on how you can answer each question. Check or look up any vocabulary which you might need.**

3 **Take turns to report to your partner.**

4 **Don't talk for more than two to three minutes each.**

5 **Debriefing:**
   • Were you each able to give your partner a good idea of the status of your work?
   • Was it easy to stick to the time frame and limit yourself to just answering the three questions?
   • Did you use chunking and pausing effectively?
   • Ask your partner one question, based on what you now know about their work.

18 Match the terms (1–4) with their definitions (a–d). How would you translate each term into German?

1 technical dinosaur
2 steep learning curve
3 tech-savvy
4 tech host

a having good knowledge and understanding of modern technology
b someone who provides technical support alongside a meeting moderator
c the situation of having to learn challenging new skills quickly
d someone who isn't up to date in terms of technological advances

 In pairs, read and discuss the comments about online meetings. To what extent do they reflect your own experience? What percentage of your work meetings and workshops take place online?

1 I'd always considered myself to be a technical dinosaur until I started working remotely.
2 Having to suddenly work from home meant a very steep learning curve for many of us.
3 Most people in my company have become surprisingly tech-savvy – because they had to!
4 I'm grateful that we have a tech host in our online workshops to help us when we need it.

19 Victoria was interviewed about her role as tech host. Complete her answer with words from the box.

breakout | individual | function | monitor | platforms | sessions | support | thread

"In online workshops, it's my role to give technical _____¹ to the facilitator and the attendees.

I prepare tools like collaboration _____² that we plan to use. Attendees are often very

tech-savvy themselves, but some need more help. During the workshops, if technical difficulties arise,

I can help _____³ participants by using the chat _____⁴ or _____⁵ rooms. It's

also my job to _____⁶ the chat and document discussions and brainstorming _____⁷.

I also add files and links to the chat _____⁸ at the appropriate time."

 Do you have experience of being a tech host or asking a tech host for help? Talk about this in pairs.

 20 During the interview, Victoria mentioned some of the most common questions she is asked. How would you respond in each case?

1 What do I have to do to share my presentation?
2 The font is too small on the document I want to share. How can I zoom in to make it easier to read?
3 How can I just share one window instead of my screen?
4 How can I customize my background image?
5 What can I do so that multiple people can collaborate on one file?

USEFUL PHRASES Giving instructions

If you're sure
- First click on … Then select …
- Make sure … is turned on.
- Right-click … on your desktop and select …
- Click on … and a drop-down menu will appear.
- Click on the … icon in the toolbar.
- … then select "Apply".

If you're not sure
- I would try to … or you could try …
- I think you do it by going to the top of your screen and then select …
- I always restart my computer and try again.
- First you have to upload the file then I think you can …
- To be honest, I can't really help you.

ENGLISH FOR TODAY'S WORKPLACE

21 Giving evidence of their green agenda is important for businesses nowadays. One way is by referring to their sustainability Key Performance Indicators (KPIs). Look at this list of environmental KPIs and discuss their relevance to your company's business activities.

carbon footprint | energy efficiency | recycling rates | waste management | water usage | supply chain sustainability

22 A meeting often includes short presentations. Share your advice for presenting effectively – and what to avoid.

23 Listen to an internal online meeting and presentation and answer the questions.

1 Where has Rosa joined the meeting from?
2 What two reasons does Liam mention for the company's interest in this potential new supplier?
3 What kind of background image is Rosa using for this meeting?
4 What does Liam offer to do while Rosa is speaking?
5 What three topics is Rosa going to cover in her presentation?
6 Which of the KPIs in exercise 21 do Rosa and Liam refer to?

Read through the Useful Phrases. Listen again and underline the phrases you hear in the Transcript on page 79.

> **USEFUL PHRASES** Presenting to colleagues during a meeting
>
> **Giving an overview of the presentation topics**
> - I'd like to cover a number of topics related to …
> - I'd like to give you a breakdown of the opportunities …
>
> **Describing the structure of a presentation**
> - I'll start with …
> - I'd like to walk you through …
> - Then I'll move on to …
> - Then finally, I'll talk about …
>
> **Describing content**
> - OK, so let me outline …
> - I think it's important to highlight the fact that …
>
> **Presenting in an online meeting**
> - Let me know if the sound quality isn't so good.
> - I'm going to share my screen …
> - Let me share the document so that you can …
> - I'll adjust the zoom settings to make it easier to read.
> - Roman will be monitoring the chat for any comments or questions you have.
>
> **Transitioning**
> - OK, let's move on to the next point.
> - This brings me to …
> - Right, now for …
>
> **Ending a presentation**
> - Let me finish by answering any questions you may have.
> - That brings me to the end of …

Choose a topic connected to your work and give a mini-presentation to the group. Use phrases from the box to signpost your talk.

24 Thinking about your own industry, company or team, use the phrases below to discuss any challenges you face.

> **USEFUL PHRASES** Talking about potential risks
> - It's highly likely that …
> - It's pretty unlikely that … unless …
> - It's possible that …
> - There's a slight chance that …
> - We have to take into account that …
> - There some hope that …
> - There's a great risk of …
> - There's very little hope of …

25 In order to deal with a problem, it's necessary to understand it thoroughly. Complete the phrases with verbs from the box. You may have to change the form of the verb.

> follow | get | mean | misunderstand | put | say | understand

1 If I _____ you correctly, the project launch is going to be delayed again.
2 So you're _____ that we're already over budget?
3 Just to be sure I haven't _____, could you explain the last point again, please?
4 Could you _____ that in other words for me? I think I missed the point.
5 I'm sorry, I didn't quite _____ your reasoning on that. Could you explain it again?
6 What I _____ to point out was that the system isn't working as we had hoped.
7 What I'm _____ at is that the deadline for submitting the report is very soon.

26 Match the sentence halves to make suggestions for dealing with problems.

1 Unfortunately we didn't anticipate that there would be so much disruption to the supply chain
2 As inflation is going to be high for the foreseeable future, I suggest
3 As we've fallen behind schedule, let's talk to the product owner
4 One way to improve our communication strategy
5 In the worst case scenario, we'll have to
6 We're dealing with too many tasks at once so I suggest

a to discuss postponing the rollout.
b implement our contingency plan and reassign the work to another factory.
c would be to tighten up our marketing messages.
d so we'll have to agree very quickly on how to work around the problem.
e revisiting our budget plan asap.
f we reprioritize and leave the least important tasks for later.

> **VOCABULARY**
> to **anticipate sth** etw. voraussehen
> to **reassign sth** hier: etw. neu zuweisen
> to **reprioritize sth** neue Prioritäten setzen
> to **revisit sth** etw. überdenken
> to **tighten sth up** etw. verschärfen, festigen

*When potential risks are identified, a **contingency plan** is developed to deal with them if necessary.*
*A **workaround** is not a planned response. It's a way of dealing with an unexpected problem.*

In pairs, take turns to tell your partner how you have addressed problems at work. Ask your partner to clarify anything you're not clear about. Use the expressions in exercises 25 and 26 for help.

ENGLISH FOR TODAY'S WORKPLACE

OVER TO YOU

 1 In pairs, discuss the items shown in the mind map and formulate a useful tip for each one. Keep your tips short and to the point.

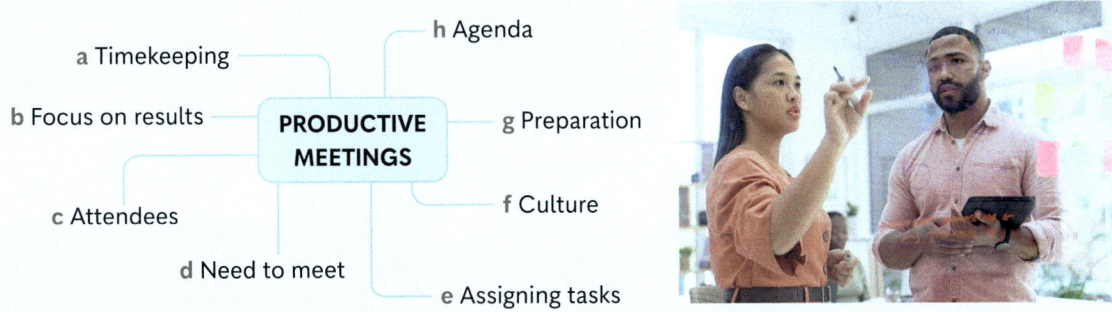

- a Timekeeping
- b Focus on results
- c Attendees
- d Need to meet
- h Agenda
- g Preparation
- f Culture
- e Assigning tasks

PRODUCTIVE MEETINGS

Share your tips with all other pairs.

 2 Match the excerpts from a meeting with the items in the mind map they reflect.

1 "Miriam, please circulate the minutes to everyone by tomorrow afternoon."
2 "Let's get started so that we don't run the risk of overrunning."
3 "My first principle is that everyone should have a voice and I'm always open to your feedback."
4 "I know you're all busy but I'm assuming everyone is ready to give their opinion on each agenda item."
5 "Is everyone in agreement with that? Great, so let's finalize our action plan."
6 "I called the meeting today because we need input from everyone before we start the first round of testing."
7 "Everyone here can contribute constructively to the items on our agenda."
8 "We can't dive too deeply into the technical issues now. That would go beyond the scope of this meeting."

 3 SIMULATION

1 In groups, use the following steps to plan the simulation.
- Decide whether you want to work on an in-person, online or hybrid meeting scenario.
- Agree on the kind of meeting culture you have.
- Assign roles according to the number of people in your group: facilitator, online participant, on-site participant, new team member, notetaker, etc.
- Think of a topic which interests you and is worth discussing in a meeting. Keep it simple!
- Write an agenda and formulate the goal of your meeting.

2 Look back through this unit and Unit 4 to check phrases you need to facilitate and participate in a meeting.

3 Check any industry-specific vocabulary you may need.

4 Debriefing
- Did everyone keep focused on the agenda topics and meeting goal?
- Did you feel confident using appropriate meeting language?
- Did you achieve your meeting goal? Why / Why not?

6   Global business speaks English

 Circle the number (1–6) to show to what extent the statements reflect your own attitudes. Compare your answers in a group.

                                                                                     agree   disagree

1. My goal is to speak English as much like a native speaker as possible.   1   2   3   4   5   6
2. For me, native speakers of English are the most difficult to understand.   1   2   3   4   5   6
3. My goal is that the people I work with understand me well enough even if my English isn't perfect.   1   2   3   4   5   6
4. It's easier to communicate in English with people who have a similar native language to your own. For example, German and Dutch or Spanish and Italian.   1   2   3   4   5   6
5. Because English is the lingua franca of international communication, we all have to be very tolerant of mistakes and try our best to understand.   1   2   3   4   5   6
6. Problems with English pronunciation are much more likely to cause communication breakdown than grammar or vocabulary mistakes.   1   2   3   4   5   6
7. Native speakers of English have an advantage in international meetings where English is the working language.   1   2   3   4   5   6
8. There are some accents I find very hard to understand.   1   2   3   4   5   6

THIS UNIT LOOKS AT ...
- the implications of using English as a lingua franca
- meetings and presentations in a global context
- the most significant intercultural issues

 1 Read the following article. With a partner, compare the information and your answers to the questionnaire.

VOCABULARY

to **estimate**   schätzen
expanding   wachsend
expansion   Erweiterung
notably   in besonderem Maße
spread   Verbreitung

Who speaks English? What kind of English do they speak?

Did you know that you are one of up to an estimated 2.3 billion people who speak English? We can divide them into three main groups: the so-called *inner circle* where English is the first language, the *outer circle*, where English is an official, second or additional language and the *expanding circle*, where English is learned as a foreign language. As the name suggests, it is the third group which is getting bigger and is having an increasing influence on the language as it evolves to suit the needs of its users. These language changes can be found in grammar, vocabulary and, most notably, in pronunciation. International intelligibility – that is using English as a shared language of communication between people from a wide range of first language backgrounds, both native-speakers and non-native speakers – is the most appropriate goal.

2 Which sounds in English are most difficult to pronounce for learners of English? Tell your partner by completing the statements below.

> I've noticed that people from … often have difficulty saying the sound …

> In my opinion, the most difficult sounds to pronounce correctly are …

18 Listen to four speakers from the expanding circle: Mieke from the Netherlands, Jonas from Austria, Akio from Japan and Camille from France. Write down what they say and discuss the following questions in pairs.

1 How confident do you feel that you understood everything?
2 Compare what you wrote. Then check the audio transcript on page 80.
3 Listen again and read the transcript at the same time until you can make out every word.
4 The mispronunciation of which sounds (if any) could lead to actual misunderstanding?

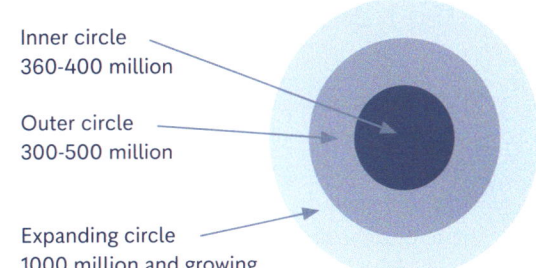

Inner circle
360-400 million

Outer circle
300-500 million

Expanding circle
1000 million and growing

3 Stressing the important words in a sentence and using a tone of voice which gives emphasis to the meaning are ways of making your message clearer to a listener. Underline the words you would stress in this conversation at a logistics company.

"Returns are just an added and unwanted cost to us. Online customers are sending more and more stuff back."
"Well, you know, you can actually save money by paying us to deal with your returns. You probably don't have the infrastructure or the staff to process returns efficiently yourself. With our logistics network, we can halve the cost for you."

> "Shall **I** call a meeting for tomorrow or do **you** want to do it?"
> "Shall I call a **meeting** for tomorrow or shall we just have a **conference call**?"

19 Listen to check the stressed words and notice the tone of voice. Check the audio transcript on page 80 if in doubt. Practise reading the conversation with your partner.

20 4 Not only accents make it difficult to understand someone. Listen to speakers from the inner and outer circle and put a cross on the line to show how well you understand each one.

	very easy to understand	very hard to understand
Speaker 1 (Murdo)		
Speaker 2 (Sarala)		

Look at the phrases below and decide what you might say to Murdo and Sarala. Add your own ideas.

USEFUL PHRASES   When you don't understand

- I'm sorry, but I didn't catch what you said.
- Could you say that again more slowly, please?
- Have I got this right? You said …
- Could you speak a bit louder, please?

- I'm sorry, my English is not so good. Did you say …?
- What was that word again?
- Believe it or not, I've never spoken to anyone from … before.
- So, do you mean …?

UNIT 6: GLOBAL BUSINESS SPEAKS ENGLISH

5 Read some comments about communicating with people whose first language is English. Share your own experience of this with a partner.

> I work in a multi-national team. We all speak good English, but the two native speakers in the team dominate our meetings so that the rest of us hardly get a word in.
>
> Elise, Brussels

> It's very difficult to understand the British guy in our team. His accent is nothing like what we learned at school – and, on top of that, he doesn't even try to speak clearly!
>
> Viviana, Bucharest

> Online meetings with our US partners are tricky because they use so many words and expressions that we've never heard before, as well as a lot of business jargon. I'm afraid we miss a lot of important details.
>
> Luca, Rome

> Everyone in our department speaks quite good English, but our Australian boss doesn't seem to have a clue what we're saying. It's very frustrating for everyone.
>
> Bai Li, Nanjing

VOCABULARY

to **get a word in** zu Wort kommen
to **not have a clue** keinen Schimmer haben
on top of that obendrein
tricky schwierig

 **6 MEDIATION**

Idioms and idiomatic phrases add variety and fun to speech, but not everyone will understand them.

1 Tell your partner 2-3 German idiomatic expressions you often use and decide together on the best translation or explanation of each one.

2 Sometimes such expressions are similar in many languages so will also be widely understood in a lingua franca context. How would you translate these into English?
   • „Wir sitzen im gleichen Boot."
   • „Man muss zwischen den Zeilen lesen"

"To get on someone's nerves" exists in no less than 57 European languages!

3 The greater a person's competence in a language, the more likely they are to know and use idiomatic expressions. In a lingua franca context, it may be a better strategy to avoid them. Reformulate the statements in exercise 5 (see: Vocabulary box) using simpler language.

4 In pairs, discuss whether you have ever used a translation app to find an English equivalent of a German idiom. How successful were you? Sometimes apps can be helpful, but not always! Look at two results and discuss which German idioms they "translate". Try to come up with more suitable English equivalents or explanations. Share your ideas in class.
   • "Caution is the mother of the china box."
   • "The knot has burst."

7 What may be a better way of expressing the meaning of these commonly used items of business jargon in a lingua franca context?

to be on the same page | to circle back | a core competency | deep dive | a game changer | to herd cats | to leverage | a no-brainer | to think outside the box | to utilize

ENGLISH FOR TODAY'S WORKPLACE

8 **In pairs, discuss whether using phrasal verbs makes your English sound more informal, more natural, and easier to understand.**

"I'll *collect* you from your hotel tomorrow." ←→ "I'll *pick* you *up* from your hotel tomorrow."

Replace the underlined verb with a phrasal verb alternative by combining a verb and a preposition from the boxes below. Adapt the form as necessary.

call | draw | find | get | go | look | put | turn   back | down | off | off | on | out | through | up

1 Can we examine (_____) these plans again together?
2 I'm afraid I'll have to postpone (_____) our meeting until next Friday.
3 The only sensible thing to do is to refuse (_____) the offer.
4 Our customers in Bahrain have cancelled (_____) their visit.
5 A lot of secret negotiations happened (_____) behind the scenes.
6 Did you discover (_____) the reason for the delay?
7 We never managed to recover (_____) the money we lost on that deal.
8 I wish you had written (_____) an agenda for this meeting.

Which alternative might be better when communicating internationally?

9 **Esther is a Kenyan engineer. Read what she says about adapting the way she speaks when using English as a lingua franca.**

"In Kenya, where English is one of the official languages, I talk about my work with people who speak English at many different levels, from native speaker competence to basic. So, I may have to ask questions to check they understand, repeat something using different words, use simpler grammar and always speak slowly and clearly. As we all work in the same industry, they may be familiar with a lot of the technical terms. Of course, if I'm speaking to foreigners, I'm careful not to use words that are only used locally! For example, do you know what a "merry-go-round" means in Kenya?"

Share your own experience of having to change the way you speak (in English, German, any other language you speak) to get your message across.

10 **Consider how you could use the following phrases to introduce something connected to your work. Take turns to talk to your partner, starting with one of the phrases.**

> **USEFUL PHRASES Preparing listeners for your next point**
>
> - I'd like to make a suggestion.
> - Just let me give my opinion on this issue.
> - I have one more question for you all.
> - I'd like to add one more point for us to consider.
> - I'd like to explain why we can't accept your offer.
> - Let's move on to talk about the progress of the project.

11 Read some posts from an online forum on working with business contacts from abroad.

Partner Files, File 5: Partner A, page 69 | Partner B, page 72

Compare the information you both found out with your own company's conventions by considering the following questions.

1 Are you on first name terms with business partners?
2 How important are business cards as part of a greeting ritual?
3 What is your policy regarding corporate gifts and entertaining?

VOCABULARY

a bribe / bribery Bestechung
lavish verschwenderisch, üppig
to **set so back** jmdn. viel Geld kosten
a token of sth *hier:* ein Zeichen von etw.

🔊 21 **Listen to three gift-giving scenarios. Think of a gift you might give a business partner and, with your partner, role play your own exchange of gifts.**

*When we talk about cultures, we are always **generalizing** to a certain degree. Behaviour may vary from person to person, company to company and from department to department within a company.*

12 Read what Ximena says about the way people prefer to communicate at her company.

"At our office in Puebla, people come over to your office all the time rather than sending an email or message. Mexicans like to talk so that always involves some informal conversation to start with! When teams work at different locations, we prefer to set up video calls. This shows we value personal relationships and other people's opinions. People may think you are impolite if you just send an email concerning an important matter without speaking about it first. An email usually just serves as confirmation. Some German colleagues based here have told me they prefer email or messaging because it's a more efficient use of their time."

*It's a good idea to know whether your partners' business culture is more **task- or people-oriented**.*

Now discuss your own communication preferences at work. Consider the following points.

close personal relationship | complicated or technical information | difficulty understanding accents | important matter | new co-worker or team member

13 In pairs, talk about making business calls. Do you start with some informal conversation or by getting straight to the point?

Read six comments from around the world. Discuss whose approach is closest to the one you prefer and what you have experienced.

If your answer to this question is "it depends", think about what the variables might be, e.g. the kind of work you do, relationship with the other person, urgency of the call, etc.

> Calls always start with some small talk irrespective of the reason for the call or who is on the call. It creates a more relaxed atmosphere. This is also true when I write emails.

Camila Machado, Brazil

> I get straight to the point. It seems impolite to waste people's time with small talk. Most people probably wouldn't know what to talk about anyway!

Morten Aaberg, Norway

> Relationships are important at work so it's only polite to start a call or an email with some small talk. But when I speak to my boss, I'm more reserved unless he starts some small talk, of course.

Mohan Kumar, India

ENGLISH FOR TODAY'S WORKPLACE

> It's pretty common to chat a bit to people you know well before moving on to the reason for the call. But it would be most unusual to talk informally with someone who has a high position in the firm.
>
> George Adeoye, Nigeria

> When speaking to people with higher level jobs than my own, I always start by asking if the person is busy and apologizing for disturbing them. Then finish by apologizing again for bothering them.
>
> Allen Chang, Taiwan

> I work in a technical department and if I speak on the phone or send an email, I always get straight to the point. I think sales staff are chattier!
>
> Andrzej Kaminski, Poland

14 In pairs, take turns to pick one of the sentences below and continue the call for as long as you can.

1. Sorry to bother you. Are you busy right now?
2. Hi (name of other person), I heard you just got back from your holiday. How was it?
3. Good morning, (your name) here. So, what's happening about the meeting next week?
4. I'm glad I caught you. I really enjoyed our talk at the trade show in Dubai.

15 Read a dictionary definition of politeness and look at two different interpretations of what this could mean in practice. What would you say to greet a latecomer to a meeting in a polite manner? Write it on the lines to the right.

politeness, *noun*:
behaviour which is socially correct and demonstrates respect and thoughtfulness towards others
(*We agreed with him, but only out of politeness.*)

> I'd just say something like, "Hi, Evan! Come on in. We started without you".
>
> Andrew

> I would only nod and not say anything at all because I wouldn't want to draw attention to them being late.
>
> Takayo

What would you say or do when ...
1. ... you notice that a colleague looks tired or sick?
2. ... your phone rings during a meeting?
3. ... a business partner repeatedly pronounces your name wrong?
4. ... a business visitor gives you their business card?
5. ... you don't understand the instructions your line manager has given you?
6. ... you have to tell a business partner that you have no time to meet them?

Compare your answers with a partner and discuss your choices. How do they align with your idea of polite behaviour? Check the Answer Key on page 88 for some examples and comments.

16 A direct communication style can sound impolite to some people. Look at the Language Focus to find ways of sounding less direct.

> **LANGUAGE FOCUS   Some softening strategies**
>
> **1** Use modal verbs (could, should, would) and make an imperative into a request.
> - *Please send me the report.* → *Could you send me the report please?*
>
> **2** Change tenses to sound more friendly.
> - *Do you have time for an online meeting today?*
>   → *I was wondering if you had time for an online meeting today.*
> - *What's your position in the company?* → *What did you say your position in the company was?*
>
> **3** Use negative questions.
> - *We should take another look at the product specifications.*
>   → *Don't you think we should take another look at the product specifications?*
>
> **4** Use vague language (not exactly, a bit, slightly, kind of, just, rather, etc.).
> - *The campaign was a disaster.* → *The campaign was a bit of a disaster.*
>
> **5** Replace negative adjectives and adverbs with "not + positive word".
> - *The kick-off meeting went badly.* → *The kick-off meeting didn't go very well.*
>
> **6** Start the sentence with a softener (I'm sorry, I'm afraid, Maybe …).
> - *I don't understand your point of view.* → *I'm afraid I don't understand your point of view.*

Think of two ways of reformulating each of these sentences to make them sound less direct.

1 Please come to my office after your lunch break.
2 Our sales figures for last year were more disappointing than we had expected.
3 We have to replace most of the equipment in our lab because it's no longer fit for purpose.
4 Be more specific.
5 We should recheck the calculations.
6 Please send me the report by Friday.
7 The project management team did a terrible job.
8 Can you arrange an earlier delivery?

17 The British have a reputation for preferring understatement and indirectness. Look at some examples and make a note of what you think the speaker may really mean.

1 It's probably my fault, but …
2 By the way, we need to talk about …
3 Please think about this again before working on …
4 That's an interesting opinion.
5 I think we have a slight problem.

Compare your ideas with a partner, then turn to the Answer Key on page 89 to check. Share any experiences you have had dealing with people who prefer an indirect communication style and discuss its pros and cons.

18 Discuss these comments about German business culture and whether they reflect your experience. Do you think they would be a good guide for someone working in Germany or do they reinforce stereotypes?

1 Yes means yes and no means no.
2 If you need help, don't wait for someone to notice, just ask.
3 Even if this sounds like a cliché, be punctual.
4 Disagreeing openly is acceptable. It's unprofessional to be vague.

19 Share an experience when it was difficult for you to keep a conversation going in English. Look at some possible reasons below and tell your partner what you think the problem was.

differences in conversation style | differences in communication style | differences in personality | language skills | lack of interest in or knowledge of the topic of conversation | lack of interest in the relationship | status difference of conversation partners

20 Work in a group of three (Partners A, B and C) and follow the instructions below.

Partners A and B
1 You are going to have a conversation. It can be work-related or not. Use your own idea or one of the ideas in the box on the right.
2 Have your conversation. Partner C is not listening out for mistakes.

challenges your industry is facing | holiday plans | latest project | sport you're interested in

Partner C
1 You are the observer. Go to the Partner Files to find out what to do.
Partner Files, File 6: page 73
2 Tell the others what you noticed.

Discuss what you think was going on at the following project meeting. The four people who attended the meeting were from Finland, Italy, Japan and Spain.

> Carlos and I were very enthusiastic about the project. I think the others were, too, but they didn't say much.
> Gianna

> The project sounds interesting, but Carlos and Gianna didn't give Tarja and me a chance to say anything.
> Kenzo

What could the participants have done to make the meeting more successful?

21 What can you say to keep your turn with business partners who commonly use overlap and speak on top of each other? Which of these sentences sound polite (P) and which are rather impolite (I)?

1 Do let me finish.
2 Just hold on.
3 Do you think I could just finish what I was saying?
4 I have one more small point so please hear me out.
5 Just give me a few more seconds.
6 I haven't finished talking yet, you know.

Mark the phrases you would feel comfortable using in an international meeting to enable and encourage quieter attendees to participate. Give reasons.

1 Marco, I must stop you here. We want to hear from everyone.
2 As the moderator, it's my role to allow everyone to speak. So, …
3 Filip, we would really appreciate hearing your views.
4 Forgive me for interrupting Jan, but you've been talking for …
5 I'd like to bring you in, Anna. What do you think?
6 Amir, you look as if you want to say something.

22 Read the advice on giving effective presentations and answer the questions below.

> The best way to deliver a message effectively is to tailor it to the people you're talking to. So, the first rule is: **know your audience!**

VOCABULARY

delivery *hier*: Vortragsweise
to tailor sth to so etw. auf jmdn. zuschneiden

1 What kinds of presentations to an external audience have you given in English?
2 What did you know about your audience? What did you do to find out more about your audience?
3 What did your audience know about you?
4 How did the knowledge you had influence your presentation, preparation, and delivery style?

Talk about your answers in a group and explain how you may vary your presentation style depending on the situation, purpose of the presentation and your audience.

23 Match the sentence halves to make phrases you can use when giving a presentation to an external audience.

1 I'm sure that what I have to tell you
2 Any input from your side
3 On behalf of my company, I'd like to
4 We have faced a number of challenges
5 I feel very confident that together
6 This takes us to the next
7 Before we move on to your questions,
8 By the end of my presentation, you'll be
9 You'll find all the details
10 My name is … and I'm delighted to be here

a to give you an overview of our e-mobility solutions.
b but we are now on track to deliver as planned.
c we can reach the goals I'll set out for you today.
d part of my talk.
e on page two of the handout.
f is particularly relevant to your own business goals.
g is most welcome so don't hesitate to interrupt me.
h welcome you to my talk.
i let me summarize the main points again.
j familiar with our plans for the new manufacturing facility.

Continue the sentence beginnings to say something about your own company's activities.

1 As you are all aware, …
2 We've made excellent progress on …
3 Despite initial setbacks in regard to …
4 I'd like to draw your attention to …
5 One of our present concerns is …
6 Our biggest success is …

24 SIMULATION

In turns, you are going to give a short presentation which is tailored to the expectations of a specific audience.

1 **Turn to the Partner Files and follow the instructions.**
   Partner Files, File 7: Partner A, page 70 | Partner B, page 73

2 **Take turns to give your presentations. Play your roles as presenter and audience member.**

3 **Debriefing**
   • Tell your partner what you noted down about the expectations of their audience. Were you right?
   • How comfortable were you presenting in your role? How was it different from your preferred style?

25 Discuss which aspects of the audience profiles reflect your own experience of presenting.

ENGLISH FOR TODAY'S WORKPLACE

OVER TO YOU

1 In pairs, discuss whether you agree with the following statement and share any examples you have experienced yourself.

> If you want to have a successful business relationship, adapt your language and behaviour to match your business partners' expectations. Don't wait for them to change theirs.

> It seems to me that we are always the ones who have to be considerate. Our business partners seem to expect us to adapt as a matter of course.

> Sometimes you just have to do what it takes if you want to close a deal, for example. Hopefully, in the long run there will be some give and take from both sides.

VOCABULARY

as a matter of course wie selbstverständlich
considerate rücksichtsvoll
to **do what it takes** tun was nötig ist
in the long run auf lange Sicht
some give and take ein gegenseitiges Geben und Nehmen

2 Listen to a podcast about working together – now and in the future. Imagine you were the guest, what would you tell Brianna about your company? Share your answer in class.

3 In pairs, talk about the specific differences in working and communication norms you have experienced at work. Describe what an ideal "third culture" could look like.

1 It's more efficient to …   2 It creates a better atmosphere when …   3 The best case would be ….

4 Global business speaks English so what impact is that having on how the language evolves? Discuss your predictions for the future of English based on this unit, your own experience and the following comments.

> **A** I read that an estimated 80% of communication in English takes place between non-native speakers.

> **B** I've noticed that we've developed our own in-house lingua franca variety of English. The main thing is that everyone understands it perfectly!

> **C** If I'm chairing an international meeting, I usually start by saying something like, "Let's speak slow English today. It's easier for all of us and will help to avoid any misunderstandings."

> **D** Do you know what "actual" and "eventual" mean? Look at the table showing "true friends" in seven European languages! Unfortunately, they're "false friends" in English – but maybe it will be their meanings in English that actually change eventually!

Czech	aktuální	eventuálně
Dutch	actueel	eventueel
French	actuel	éventuel
German	aktuell	eventuell
Polish	aktualny	ewentualny
Spanish	actual	eventual
Swedish	aktuell	eventuellt

PARTNER FILES

PARTNER A

File 1 UNIT 1 Exercise 15

Step 1: Choose one of the following small talk topics and start a conversation with your partner.

food | sport | travel | the weather

Step 2: Now change roles. Your partner will start a conversation with you. Talk about the topic for a short time. When there is a slight pause in the conversation or when you think it is a good opportunity, suggest you get down to business. Check the Useful Phrases on page 13 for some ideas of what to say.

Step 3: When you have finished both conversations, discuss how easy it was to find the right time to change the focus. Did you and your partner sound friendly and positive when you tried to change the subject?

File 2 UNIT 3 Exercise 20

Topic of the telephone call: your team's last online meeting

You call your partner. You are working from home. You would like them to summarize what happened at the last team online meeting because you were unable to attend. It is urgent because you need to know some figures to prepare some documents for your team leader. Make up any details as you go along.

During the call, the following problems arise:
- There's a lot of background noise because the builders are working on the house next door so you don't hear everything your partner says. For some reason, your partner is speaking very quietly.
- Your children have just come home from school and want their lunch so you are in a hurry to finish the call.
- Your partner uses words you don't understand.
- You have a lot of other important work to do today.

File 3 UNIT 4 Exercise 12

Read the German company policy on sustainability and prepare to explain the main points to your partner in English. Make notes on the points you want to mention but don't write a complete text in English. Keep it simple!

Klimaschutz ist das Thema der Stunde, deshalb möchten wir als Unternehmen nachhaltiger arbeiten. Nicht nur das Klima profitiert davon, sondern ebenso unser Image und Geldbeutel. Wir wollen vorbereitet sein, wenn neue Regeln und Gesetze für Klimaschutz in Kraft treten.

Hier ein Überblick über einige Maßnahmen, die wir bereits umgesetzt haben.

Verkehrsmittel:
- Durch die Einführung von digitalem Arbeiten, können unsere Teams öfter von zu Hause arbeiten. Unsere Mitarbeiter*innen müssen nicht mehr täglich pendeln.
- Wir fördern die Idee, öffentliche Verkehrsmittel für den Weg zur Arbeit zu nutzen, indem wir die Kosten der Fahrttickets unserer Mitarbeiter*innen komplett übernehmen.
- Wir haben Dienstfahrräder gekauft – für die Umwelt und für die Gesundheit unserer Belegschaft.

Im Büro:
- Wir reduzieren unseren Papierverbrauch so weit wie möglich und streben an, ein papierloses Unternehmen zu werden.
- Von Sensorgeräten bis zu smarten Steckdosen benutzen wir moderne Technologie, um unseren Energieverbrauch zu reduzieren.

File 4   UNIT 5   Exercise 1

Step 1: Read the information about two of the search results on rules for effective meetings.
Step 2: With your partner, take turns to explain what the numbers mean.
Step 3: Compare the explanations to the ones you discussed. Were you correct?
Step 4: Discuss the rules. Consider the following questions.
- What is your opinion of the suggestions?
- Do they make sense to you?
- Do you already implement them or would you want to?

A   The 40-20-40 rule
This rule says you should spend …
- 40% of your attention on meeting preparation.
- 20% on the meeting itself.
- 40% of your attention on executing the meeting action plan.

This means that 80% of making a meeting successful happens before and after the meeting, making it difficult to do if you have many back-to-back meetings.

B   The rule of 7
This rule is about the number of people who should be in a meeting to make it effective. The best number depends on the purpose of the meeting.

For problem-solving / collaborative decision-making meetings, keep the number of attendees to seven or fewer. More people usually result in lower-quality decisions.

File 5   UNIT 6   Exercise 11

Read some posts from an online forum on international business interactions. Prepare to tell your partner what you found out.

Lisa from Shanghai
In my experience, staff in companies which operate internationally always use what we call Western names. It's a kind of company rule. When I started working for a Canadian company here in Shanghai, my boss asked me for my English name on the very first day. Many foreigners find Chinese names difficult to pronounce and spell so English names are more convenient. We often choose names which sound similar to our Chinese names. My real name is Lisha, for example. In Chinese we put the family name first, then the given name. But when we use an English name it's different. My Western name is Lisa Guo, but in Chinese it's Guo Lisha!

Akio from Hiroshima
In general, Japanese people are very keen on using new technology, but one area where we are still pretty traditional is that we prefer printed business cards, not digital ones. The protocol usually goes something like this. Before the meeting you should take the number of cards you will need out of your card holder. You must have one! It's rather rude to keep cards in your pocket or wallet. As a visitor, you should offer your card first. Introduce yourself when you offer the card. And remember – always give and receive the cards with both hands. When you take someone else's card, it's polite to confirm their name and make a comment about the company or its business. Then keep the cards on the table during the meeting – and never write anything on a card! Usually, people place the cards to show who is who around the table. This is a good way of learning the names. Of course, one side of the card is printed in Japanese and the other side in English!

PARTNER FILES

File 7   UNIT 6   Exercise 24

You as the presenter

Step 1: You are going to give a short presentation based on something you mentioned about your company's activities in exercise 23. You have done some research on the expectations of your audience and have come up with the following information.

Your audience …
- expects you to start with some friendly and informal small talk.
- isn't very interested in your own background or the history of the company.
- is interested in how what you tell them is relevant to their own business.
- wants to hear a few technical details.
- expects you to interact with them on a personal level during the presentation – ask them questions, ask for comments, etc.

Step 2: Take some time to decide on the topic and your content. Prepare to speak for about 5 minutes.
Step 3: Review the phrases in exercise 23 and the Useful Phrases in Unit 5, page 55 that will be useful for the required presentation style.
Step 4: Welcome your audience and give your presentation.

You as a member of the audience

Step 1: Your role is to guess the expectations of the audience your partner has prepared to speak to. During the presentation, make a few notes on these expectations.
Step 2: Listen attentively to your partner's presentation and interact with them as necessary.

PARTNER B

File 1   UNIT 1   Exercise 15

Step 1: Your partner will start a conversation with you. Talk about the topic for a short time. When there is a slight pause in the conversation or when you think it is a good opportunity, suggest you get down to business. Check the Useful Phrases on page 13 for some ideas of what to say.
Step 2: Now change roles. Choose one of the following small talk topics and start a conversation with your partner.

health | hometown | music | weekend

Step 3: When you have finished both conversations, discuss how easy it was to find the right time to change the focus. Did you and your partner sound friendly and positive when you tried to change the subject?

File 2   UNIT 3   Exercise 20

Topic of the telephone call: your team's last online meeting

You attended the meeting but your partner didn't. Your partner calls you. You are on a train when you get the call. Answer your partner's questions as best you can. Make up any details as you go along.

During the call, the following problems arise:
- You are on the train and you lose the connection from time to time.
- You try to speak quietly because some of the information your partner is asking you for is highly confidential. Also, some of your fellow travellers are looking at you in an annoyed way.
- Your partner is speaking very quickly so you often don't catch what they say.
- You notice that your battery is getting low and your charging cable is somewhere in your luggage.

File 3   UNIT 4   Exercise 12

Read the German company policy on "back-to-the-office" and prepare to explain the main points to your partner in English. Make notes on the points you want to mention but don't write a complete text in English. Keep it simple!

Das Homeoffice und hybrides Arbeiten haben sich in unserer Arbeitswelt etabliert und werden auch in Zukunft nicht verschwinden. Wir möchten aber, dass unsere Mitarbeiter*innen sich mit dem Unternehmen verbunden fühlen, weshalb wir eine Strategie entwickelt haben, die wir „Rückkehr ins Büro" nennen.

Hier einige Eckpunkte:
- Wir merken, dass der direkte Austausch mit Kolleg*innen unseren Mitarbeiter*innen sehr wichtig geblieben ist.
- Wir erkennen, dass Büroräume anders genutzt werden als früher und haben deshalb alle Flächen umgestaltet.
- Wenn wir Meetings im Büro planen, kombinieren wir sie mit einem Team-Frühstück oder Lunch.
- Wir bieten eine Auswahl an Räumen an, in denen Mitarbeiter*innen konzentriert arbeiten können, als auch Räume für gemeinschaftliches Arbeiten und soziale Kontakte.
- Wir bitten regelmäßig um Feedback und Anregungen und berücksichtigen so viel wie möglich, wenn Entscheidungen anstehen.

PARTNER FILES

File 4   UNIT 5   Exercise 1

Step 1: Read the information about two of the search results on rules for effective meetings.
Step 2: With your partner, take turns to explain what the numbers mean.
Step 3: Compare the explanations to the ones you discussed. How close were you?
Step 4: Discuss the rules. Consider the following questions.
- What is your opinion of the suggestions?
- Do they make sense to you?
- Do you already implement them or would you want to?

A The 10-10-10 rule
This rule is a decision-making technique which encourages you to think of the consequences of a decision. When you consider a decision, ask yourself what the consequences will be in 10 minutes, in 10 months and in 10 years.

B The 5 second rule
This rule is for meeting facilitators.

When you ask a question, wait for a full five seconds before moving on. For example, when you ask if there are any more questions, wait five seconds to show that you welcome a response of some kind. By this time the silence becomes a little uncomfortable and people will usually start to respond.

File 5   UNIT 6   Exercise 11

Read some posts from an online forum on international business interactions. Prepare to tell your partner what you found out.

Anders from Oslo
Norway doesn't have a gift-giving business culture, but we might give business partners small gifts, generally at the end of successful negotiations and maybe something with our company logo on it. A present should never look like a bribe! As far as entertaining visitors is concerned, we like to take people out to see our beautiful landscapes. Business gifts and entertaining should never cost too much money and our company actually sets limits on the sums we are allowed to spend on entertaining. Norway is an expensive place to live so even a meal in a nice restaurant can set you back quite a lot!

Leo Chen from Suzhou
In the past, companies gave expensive gifts to business partners and spent lavishly on entertaining visitors. It was not uncommon to take guests on expensive trips, for example. It's still very important to build relationships before doing business here so we go to nice restaurants and book a separate room just for our group. It's no longer allowed to give individuals expensive gifts in case it looks like a bribe. We always take gifts, but for the whole department we're visiting. We generally choose something rather traditional to represent our local culture or something connected to Chinese history.

Khalid from Abu Dhabi
All over the Middle East there's a strong tradition of gift-giving in personal and professional life. So I suppose business people here expect their visitors to bring a gift of some sort! The gifts we give most frequently are local specialities – sweets and pastries for example. So, nothing too lavish, but as a token of the importance of the relationship. If your company's policy doesn't allow giving and receiving gifts, it's best to tell your partners so that nobody loses face.

File 7   UNIT 6   Exercise 24

You as the presenter

Step 1: You are going to give a short presentation based on something you mentioned about your company's activities in exercise 23 You have done some research on the expectations of your audience and have come up with the following information.

Your audience …
- expects you to show respect to them and mention positive impressions of their country.
- is very interested in the history and reputation of your company.
- wants to know something about your own professional background.
- is more interested in the big picture than technical details.
- expects you to offer one-to-one talks with anyone who is interested after the presentation.

Step 2: Take some time to decide on the topic and your content. Prepare to speak for about 5 minutes.
Step 3: Review the phrases in exercise 23 and the Useful Phrases in Unit 5, page 55 that will be useful for the required presentation style.
Step 4: Welcome your audience and give your presentation.

You as a member of the audience

Step 1: Your role is to guess the expectations of the audience your partner has prepared to speak to. During the presentation, make a few notes on these expectations.
Step 2: Listen attentively to your partner's presentation and interact with them as necessary. If you have a question, you can ask.

PARTNER C

File 6   UNIT 6   Exercise 20

Step 1: You are observing the others to find out their turn-taking behaviour. Make notes on the following.
- How often does either partner interrupt the other – if at all?
- Are there silent pauses during the conversation when nobody speaks? If so, how long are these pauses?
- If there are periods of silence, does either partner seem uncomfortable?

Step 2: Prepare to explain to the others what your task was and what you observed.

TRANSCRIPTS

UNIT 1   Exercise 3

 02

Conversation 1
Lena: Good morning, Mr Johnson. We're so pleased, you could finally come over.
Sean: Great to be here – and please call me Sean. And you must be Lena Seitz. I think we were on a video call together, right? It was a long time ago.
Lena: Yes, that's right, I think we were. Let's go and sit down over here for a moment. Can I get you a coffee or something else to drink, Sean? Johann just texted me to say he'll be down in a moment.
Sean: A glass of mineral water would be perfect. I had a huge breakfast with too much coffee at the hotel. You found a wonderful hotel for me, Lena!
Lena: Glad to hear that. The hotel does have a good name around here. I'll just go and get your drink. By the way, the restrooms are over there on the right.

Conversation 2
Giulia: Hello everyone. It's great to see you all on the call today because I'd like to give Alessandro the chance to find out who's who in our project team. Here he is, sitting next to me. He works with me in the Milan office and will be part of our team from now on. So, let's start with a short round of introductions so he knows who you all are and what your roles are. Go ahead, Matt.
Matt: Hi everyone, and pleased to meet you Alessandro. I'm Matt, as you just heard. I'm based in Manchester – in the UK Sales Division. Welcome to the team! We're looking forward to working with you.
Giulia: Thanks, Matt. So, who's going next? How about you, Helen? …

Conversation 3
Stephan: Good morning, Mr Liu. Stephan Scholz here. Don't worry, I'm already at the station. Can you tell me which platform you're on?
Liu: Hello Mr Scholz – no problem. My train arrived a bit early, in fact. I'm standing on platform eleven.
Stephan: I'm sorry, I didn't quite catch the number. Was it seven or eleven?
Liu: Platform eleven.
Stephan: OK, I'm nearly there, so please just stay where you are and I'll be with you in a few moments. …
Sorry to keep you waiting. I couldn't find a parking space in front of the station. Anyway, welcome to Augsburg. Let me help you with your bags.
Liu: Thanks, that's very kind!
Stephan: So how was your trip? I think you stayed overnight in Munich before coming on to Augsburg, right?

Liu: Yes, that's right. In fact, I stayed there for two nights because I wanted to visit an old friend who lives there. I didn't want to miss that opportunity!
Stephan: Of course not! My car's this way. I expect you'd like to go to your hotel first of all?
Liu: Yes, please. I think that …

Conversation 4
Emma: I don't think we've met before, have we? May I introduce myself? I'm Emma Wentworth – I'm based in Stuttgart at the moment. Please call me Emma, by the way.
Kasia: Hello Emma. And I suppose working for that world-famous automotive company! I'm Katarzyna, Katarzyna Kaminska.
Emma: You're quite correct about my job! Nice to meet you Katarzyna. Am I pronouncing your name correctly?
Kasia: Well, why don't you just call me Kasia?
Emma: OK, thanks Kasia. I can see from your name tag that you work in Germany, too.
Kasia: Yes, very near Wolfsburg. I'm working on autonomous systems for the automotive industry. It's fascinating work.
Emma: I'd love to hear more about that. Shall we pick up a coffee before the next talk?
Kasia: Good idea. There's some just over there.

UNIT 1   Exercise 11

 03

1
Speaker A: That's your job, I suppose.
Speaker B: That's your job, I suppose.

2
Speaker A: That sounds good.
Speaker B: That sounds good.

3
Speaker A: Oh really?
Speaker B: Oh really?

UNIT 1   Exercise 20

04

Conversation 1
Host: I can hear the catering staff setting up our lunch outside so I think it's time to have something to eat. We need a break anyway! You'll see that the plates of vegetarian and vegan food are clearly labelled. So please help yourselves!
Guest: This looks delicious. It's a good idea to have a light lunch so we don't all fall asleep!

Host: We thought so, too, and anyway, we're going out to a very nice restaurant this evening. ... Why don't you try this? It tastes very good – as long as you like spicy food, that is.
Guest: Is it very spicy? I have to be a bit careful about ...

Conversation 2
Jos: So, here we are, Asma. Don't bother reading the menu – just come and have a look.
Asma: That's a good idea.
Jos: This is what's on offer today. All the food is halal, by the way. We always have one fish dish, one meat dish and a vegetarian option. There are a few starters, and sandwiches and desserts, too.
Asma: Oh, there's a good choice of dishes. It all looks quite delicious, but, you know, Jos, I'm not very hungry so can I ask for a small portion?
Jos: Yes, sure. The trays are right here and we can pick up knives and forks over there. If you need any help, just ask me but I think all the staff speak English.

Conversation 3
Lauren: Well, let's have a look at the menu. By the way, do either of you have any food allergies? I can call the server over and ask them about the ingredients.
Clémence: No, not me. What about you, Oliver?
Oliver: No, fortunately I'm not allergic to anything. This is an impressive menu. Hmm, I'm really not sure what to choose. What would you recommend, Lauren?
Lauren: Well, I'm a vegetarian and I try something different every time I come here! But, in fact, the signature dish at this restaurant is an Argentinian specialty. The chef is from Buenos Aires. Would you like to have that, Oliver? Clémence?
Clémence: I'd love to try it.
Olivier: Me, too. Especially as it's something we can only eat here.
Lauren: OK, so that's settled. Now what would you both like to drink?
Clémence: What are you having, Lauren?
...
Lauren: So, how was the meal? Was everything all right?
Oliver: It was delicious. Thanks for the recommendation.
Lauren: Excellent. So, who's for a dessert?
Clémence: I really couldn't manage another mouthful.
Oliver: Well, since you're asking ... I always have room for a dessert.

UNIT 2   Exercise 4

🔊 05

Hi everyone! How many work emails did you write or receive yesterday? I'm guessing quite a lot because we rely heavily on emails to communicate with others in our jobs. So today, I'd like to give you my top tips for writing effective emails which share information clearly and don't go on for paragraphs!
Number one is probably obvious, but I'm going to say it anyway – make sure your subject line really matches the content. This might make the difference between the recipient actually reading the email or not!
The second tip is to focus on one topic – the one in the subject line – and keep the email short and the language simple. Only use vocabulary which you are pretty sure the person you're writing to will understand.
Number three is to start and finish your email in a friendly way – for example, by thanking the writer. asking how they are or wishing them well. The way you start an email sets the tone for the whole thing and can immediately make a positive or negative impression on the reader. A bit of small talk to start is often a good idea unless you are writing a very formal email.
My fourth tip is a very important one. Anyone can forward your email to other people so watch your words! An email is a written record of your conversation so don't write anything you wouldn't want put on the record. Be especially careful that you don't write something in an email which could cause legal problems for you or your company.
I'd like to say a word here about using artificial intelligence or machine translations to create emails. These are tools which can be very useful to develop your own writing skills as well as saving time, but never feed confidential personal or corporate information into these tools.
The next tip is a very important one! Sending out emails with typos and mistakes of any kind makes you look unprofessional, so please do take the time to proofread what you've written. My motto is – if in doubt, check again! Another point is that it's not only about "mistakes" in your writing – make sure you stick to the same tone and style, so for example, don't write a mix of formal and informal or friendly and reserved language.
My sixth – and final – tip is to collect sentences, words or phrases you see in well-written emails and create your own templates to re-use them yourself in the future. However, when you do this, proofread everything very carefully before you copy and paste it into your own collection. It's not only a question of

accuracy but also making sure you are using language which is suitable for the situation.

So that's it, but I'd be very happy to know what you think about my six top tips so please post a comment if you have time. And if you would like to share any of your own tips – even better!

UNIT 2 Exercise 17

 06

Javid: As you can imagine, AI is a huge topic at the conference so I decided to interview a few people on one aspect of it – how they use AI and machine translation in general in everyday business communication. I made a few recordings while I was walking around. The first person I spoke to was Liliana from Brno in the Czech Republic. This is what she said.

Liliana: Well, if I'm writing an email in English to a client, I usually use a machine translation app to check my spelling and grammar – especially if I'm a bit unsure of something. I don't often find mistakes actually, but it just makes me feel more confident that I'm sending professional emails to my clients. Translation tools have become so much better, but, of course, I always read the sentences again very carefully because I don't trust them 100%! You know, there's a risk that the tone or the style might not be what I want. But, generally speaking, a machine translation app is a very useful way of improving my own texts by showing me phrases I wouldn't have thought of using and helping me to spot mistakes.

Javid: That sounds pretty typical to me of how people use machine translation these days. The next person I spoke to was Eduardo. He works in the automotive industry in Puebla, Mexico. This is what he told me.

Eduardo: There's so much hype about AI-powered chatbots, right? So, I had to try it out! Of course, you can create emails in seconds – and that's brilliant because sometimes it takes me ages to write one myself! However, the quality depends on the background information the user provides and the suitability of the prompts so I think very carefully about what exactly I want to say. Often enough, I send an email to a client and then a few moments later set up a video call with them. So, this means I really have to know what was in the email! There's no question in my mind that I can save a lot of time with the help of AI. Of course, I still need to improve my English because a lot of the time, I'm in online meetings, talking to clients and business partners. I don't think they want to talk to a robot!

One thing that worries me a bit, though, is the legal situation – if I let AI create a text for me, who does it belong to?

Javid: That was interesting, right? Then the next person I spoke to was Tobias. He's an engineer from Karlsruhe in Germany.

Tobias: Some of my emails contain very technical language which requires very specialized terminology as well as an understanding of the subject matter. I've noticed that machine translations don't always identify the context correctly, but I suppose that's not surprising. Anyway, I don't use AI-based tools for emails like this. When it comes to more straight-forward requests or information-sharing with clients – things like that – I am using AI more and more. For me, these tools are also a convenient way to learn new words and phrases and improve my grammar – with the bonus of saving time, of course.

UNIT 3 Exercise 3

 07

Vladimir: Good morning. This is Vladimir Karpov from SOP.

Alena: Good morning, Mr Karpov. Alena Novak speaking. How can I help you?

Vladimir: I'm calling about the fabric sample you sent us last week. It worked well in tests in the lab, but there are still a few open questions.

Alena: I'm glad to hear that the test was successful. Are your questions about the technology or about delivery terms, cost, and so on?

Vladimir: Well, first of all about the technology. We can leave the other things for later. As you know, we manufacture airbags and we're working on an air bag which is smaller and not so heavy. Well, I have a question about the coating of the fabric …

Alena: Excuse me, Mr Karpov. Sorry to interrupt you, but may I say something? I think you should speak to Sergio personally about this. He's in a meeting at the moment, but I'll tell him you called and ask him to phone you back as soon as possible.

Vladimir: OK, then. I'd like to speak to him as soon as I can, so when do you think he might be …

UNIT 3 Exercise 7

 08

Message 1
Good morning, Jan, this is Tomas. I'm calling about the list of special offers for our premium customers we spoke about yesterday. Could you email me the latest figures by tomorrow morning, please? Thanks.

Message 2
Hello Jan, this is Julia Chen speaking. I'd like to have confirmation that you have changed the hotel booking for our delegation. Could you send it to me as soon as you hear this, please? We need it to apply for our visas. I'll call again later – at 3 pm your time because there are a few other things we should talk about. Speak soon.

Message 3
Hi, Jan, Martin here. I'm ringing about the email you sent me yesterday. The date and time you suggest for a web meeting is OK with me. Do you already have an agenda? If so, could you send it by Tuesday morning? If you want to discuss the agenda first, just call me on my mobile. Thanks.

UNIT 3 Exercise 14

09

Anna: Hi Jeppe. It can't be eleven thirty, surely? I've only just got into the office.
Jeppe: Hi Anna. No, no it's only ten fifteen. I'm sorry to have to call you now, but something has come up. I'm afraid that I'll have to reschedule our phone call. A client has brought forward an appointment we had for this afternoon.
Anna: Oh well, things like that can happen. No worries. So, what do you suggest? Could we talk later today or shall we postpone the call until next week?
Jeppe: Thanks for being so understanding. I'm really sorry about this. If it works for you, shall we reschedule for Monday morning at nine?
Anna: Yeah, that suits me – but promise me that I won't be in the office at nine on Monday for nothing!
Jeppe: Anna, you're the best!

UNIT 3 Exercise 19

 10

1 A: I'd like to speak to Ms Martínez, please.
  B: Please hold on. I'll put you through.
2 A: Philip isn't in the office today.
  B: Well that's a pity. Could I leave a message for him, please?
3 A: Oh hello, I didn't recognize your voice.
  B: Oh, I'm not surprised. I've got a terrible cold.
4 A: Is this a good time to talk?
  B: Well, I have a meeting in a few minutes, but go ahead.
5 A: She's in a meeting now. I think she'll be available after lunch.
  B: OK, then I'll try again later.
6 A: I'm returning your call.
  B: That's great. I have a few things I'd like to discuss with you.

UNIT 3 Exercise 27

 11

Lydia: Lydia Anderson speaking. Hello Mr Hansen. Thank you for calling back at such short notice. How's the weather in Munich now? Pretty cold, I expect.
Fritz: Hello Ms Anderson. Actually, I'm in Vienna today – and yes, it's pretty cold here, too! Anyway, I don't want to take up too much of your time. I understand you want to find out more about the latest model of our civilian drones.
Lydia: Yes, that's right. Basically, I need to know what's different about the new drone.
Fritz: Well, they can get much …
Lydia: Hello? You're breaking up. Mr Hansen, are you still there?
Fritz: Yes, I'm sorry. The signal is very poor at the moment.
Lydia: I'm afraid I didn't catch the last thing you said.
Fritz: Well, I was saying they can get much closer to buildings and the camera quality is far better. The live images are really excellent. You know, I'd like to make a suggestion. I'm in the UK in two weeks – why don't I come to Manchester so we can talk in more detail?
Lydia: Brilliant! Let me check my schedule. Would Tuesday, the 7th of November work for you?
Fritz: That sounds like an …

TRANSCRIPTS

UNIT 4   Exercise 6

🔊 12

Antonia: So have you just moved to Bonn?
Dominic: Oh, I don't live here. I was looking for a job which allowed me to work from home because I don't feel like moving house – again! I've just returned to Germany from working for a few years back in Dublin. I live in Darmstadt now.
Antonia: I know just what you mean about moving! Well, let me show you around the building first so you can see where you'll be working and what facilities you can use whenever you do come in. So, take a look around – it's changed so much since I joined the company five years ago. We're changing our office space to optimize the design for our present needs. For one thing, we've reduced our capacity because there are never more than 50% of staff on-site at one time. Most people join meetings online.
Dominic: Aren't there any private offices at all now?
Antonia: Basically, it's only top management who has a private office. Some managers share offices, but everyone else sits in these open areas. If you look over there, you'll see one of the hot-desking benches. We have at least one area like that on each floor.
Dominic: Umm. I suppose we use a desk-booking system if we plan to come in.
Antonia: Yeah, that's right. I'm sure you're familiar with that from your last job. There are open areas for informal meetings dotted around the office – here and over there in the corner.
Dominic: Ah, yes. I don't mind working in a busy environment from time to time. It can be a bit too quiet in my home office!
Antonia: I feel the same – but I always have my headphones with me here in case the conversations around me get too lively. Of course, we have silent pods – the ones that look like telephone booths – for making phone calls or for working alone. Let's go and have a look, shall we? There's a vacant one over there. You can't book those in advance so you just have to take your chances on getting one!
Dominic: Are there quiet zones, too? In my last job, there was an area of the office dedicated to working in silence – no phones and no conversations.
Antonia: Yes, the quiet zone on this floor is round the corner – more secluded and far away from the restrooms and the kitchen. There are also a few booths there if people do need to talk. So let me show you the silent pod first and then we can walk over to the quiet zone. On tiptoe, of course! So, look, this is the …

UNIT 4   Exercise 9

🔊 13

Max: The topic I'd like to talk about today / is our company's work phone policy. // The starting point / is that we allow / and even encourage staff to work remotely / so we need a policy to manage this effectively. // One very important issue for us / if not the most important / is data security. // That's the reason why all staff who have access to confidential company data / are given company-owned phones. // By the way, we call this COBO. // That stands for company owned, / business only. // The company has complete control over all the apps on the phone, / all the data, / and the device itself. // I'd also like to mention another option / and that is BYOD. // That means Bring Your Own Device / and also has advantages. // So, how does this work? // Well …

UNIT 4   Exercise 17

🔊 14

Patrick Campbell: Wang gong, hen kai xin wo jin tian neng gou lai dao zhe le.
Mr Wang: Campbell xian sheng, wo bu zhi dao nin …
Patrick Campbell: Oh, excuse me Mr Wang. Excuse me, I'm afraid I don't speak Chinese. My colleague Andrea just taught me a few words to greet you with!
Mr Wang: Ah, yes, I remember her. She speaks excellent Chinese. But I must say, your accent is already very good!
Patrick Campbell: Oh well – I tried my best.
Mr Wang: Well, let's go back to English! May I ask you to please keep together at all times. We don't want to lose anybody. … Right, here we are. Before we go in, please put on the protective clothing. … Just over on the left, you can see the entrance to our R&D lab. So, let's go in.
Patrick Campbell: Thank you. I'm sure I'm going to have a lot of questions.
Mr Wang: Feel free to ask! … If everyone has had the chance to see everything here, shall we head over to the second production hall? … Right. This is where we manufacture parts for trucks. We were talking about this over coffee.
Patrick Campbell: Mmm. You mentioned earlier that this line has the most downtime, right?
Mr Wang: Yes, unfortunately, but the equipment is no longer state-of-the-art to be quite honest with you, so we're replacing it very shortly.
Patrick Campbell: I see. How long does it take to retool the line when you switch to the new technology?

Mr Wang: Um, not very long. I think two weeks at most.
Patrick Campbell: That sounds impressive!
Mr Wang: Well, we have full order books so we can't afford to lose too much time. Let's move on, shall we? Before we finish the tour, we should walk over to the quality control department.
Patrick Cambell: That sounds like an excellent idea. …
Mr Wang: Well, that's all we have time for today. Let's make our way back to the conference room. I'm sure that some refreshments are waiting for us!

UNIT 5 Exercise 3

🔊 15

Speaker 1: Let's get started, shall we? We need to come up with some new ideas on how we can improve sales.

Speaker 2: Pedro, I can't see you. Can you turn on your video, please?

Speaker 3: As this is our first meeting, shall we start by everyone introducing their role in the project?

Speaker 4: OK, so we've identified a few things we could have done better. Anything else before we move on?

UNIT 5 Exercise 15

🔊 16

Jessica: OK, my phone says 9 o'clock so let's start. We want to hear what you did, what you're doing, and any obstacles. Please sidebar anything else so it doesn't hold us up. Rohan, why don't you start?
Marta: Just a minute, Jessica. Maxim hasn't arrived yet.
Jessica: I know, but you know our meeting guidelines and time is short. So, Rohan, what did you do yesterday?
Rohan: Right. Yesterday, I worked with Gregor on the sales figures which have come in from the car dealerships. We double-checked everything and finished the spreadsheet so it's ready to be distributed to the team. And today, I'm formulating our takeaways from the figures – they're looking good, by the way – and then I'll be sending round the spreadsheet and our comments so that everyone is up to speed.
Jessica: Great. That sounds like progress because we need that data to move forward. Any obstacles you're dealing with?

Rohan: Not for what I have to do today, but I've been trying to reach out to Jason at the software developers. I've had no response whatsoever. There are a few issues I have to discuss with him very soon or this will completely block my progress down the line. Has anyone else had the same problem?
Marta: In fact, I spoke to Jason the day before yesterday. As far as I understood him, they're having a few problems with …
Jessica: Thanks Marta, sorry to interrupt, but can you speak to Rohan later to fill him in with what's going on there. Maybe you can both hang around after this meeting?
Marta: Sure. No problem.
Jessica: There have been a lot of problems with the developers, but I think we should sidebar that for now. Thanks, Rohan. Now let's move on to …

UNIT 5 Exercise 23

🔊 17

Liam: Right, so let's move on to the next item on the agenda – Rosa's visit to a potential new supplier in Porto. She's there at the moment and will give us her first impressions. She'll be joining the meeting shortly. While we're waiting for her, let me just say that the company would be able to supply high-end leather shoes as well as various sports shoes. If we go ahead, we could replace our dependency on our Chinese and Italian suppliers. So, we'll … ah, here she is. Good morning, Rosa.
Rosa: Good morning from Porto. I've changed my background image for the meeting so you can enjoy Porto, too!
Liam: We're quite envious!
Rosa: Right, I'd like to cover a number of topics related to our plan to work with our new supplier. I'll start with sustainability issues. After all, that's one of the main reasons why we're thinking of switching suppliers. Then I'll move on to talk about the products and the manufacturing plant itself.
Liam: Can I come in here, Rosa? I suggest writing any comments or questions in the chat. I'll be monitoring it while Rosa is speaking.
Rosa: Thanks, Liam. Good idea. As I think you all know, part of my brief for the visit was to understand how the manufacturer would help us tackle our environmental KPIs. I'd like to walk you through the KPIs we've chosen for … Let's move on to the next point – how our new supplier can help us cover the main issues. I'm going to share my screen again so you can see the relevant points. Let's start with materials and recycling rates. They work closely with their suppliers to ensure that …

TRANSCRIPTS

Then we reviewed the areas we need to address to make our supply chain greener, the weight of packaging – of the products and secondary packaging on pallets and in containers.
Liam: May I come in here again, Rosa?
Rosa: Go ahead.
Liam: One benefit of focusing on a supplier who can provide the complete range of products we need is in the transportation. This way, larger quantities can be shipped at one time and the distance is shorter and we won't have to use road transport. This will certainly have a positive effect on our carbon-footprint. ...
Rosa: So, that brings me to the end of the first part. Let me finish by answering any questions you may have – please fire away. Oh, and I think, Roman, you've picked up some comments and questions from the chat ...

UNIT 6 Exercise 2

🔊 18
Mieke: It's time to hear some facts and figures about the company.
Jonas: And now we have more than 300 jobs all over the world.
Kazuo: We think it is very rude to give your opinion directly.
Camille: I hope to see you this afternoon.

UNIT 6 Exercise 3

🔊 19
Speaker 1: <u>Returns</u> are just an <u>added</u> and <u>unwanted cost</u> to us. <u>Online</u> customers are sending <u>more and more</u> stuff back.

Speaker 2: Well, you know, you can actually <u>save money</u> by paying <u>us</u> to deal with your returns. You probably don't have the <u>infrastructure</u> or the <u>staff</u> to process returns efficiently yourself. With our <u>logistics network</u>, we can <u>halve</u> the cost for you.

UNIT 6 Exercise 4

🔊 20
Speaker 1: People who think they already speak English and know that Scotland is an English-speaking country expect communication here to be easy. But when they come to Glasgow, they're in for a shock. Great town though.

Speaker 2: English is the second official language of India, but I don't think you can say that there's one kind of Indian English. For example, a person's accent depends on his or her first language, and India has hundreds of different languages and dialects.

UNIT 6 Exercise 11

🔊 21
Scenario 1
Ole: Remember I told you about everyone in Norway's favourite cheese the last time I was here?
Janet: Er, yes, I think I do. There was something special about it, wasn't there?
Ole: That's right. Well, here it is. I've brought you some so that you can try it for yourself. Look it's brown and it has a kind of caramel taste, it's slightly sweet – and it's something typically Norwegian.
Janet: Thank you, Ole. I love trying new kinds of food. I'll let you know how I like it.

Scenario 2
Ashton: By the way, here's a small gift from Mr Jenner. He told me he played golf with you the last time he was here and asked me to give it to you.
Andreas: Thanks, Ashton. Yes, we did play, I remember. He's a very good player. Maybe this will bring me better luck when I play against him next time!
Ashton: Let's hope so. You can imagine why all our corporate gifts have something to do with golf!

Scenario 3
Jiang Jing: On behalf of my company, I'd like to present you with this very traditional gift. Please go ahead and open it.
Steven: Oh, thank you. It's beautiful.
Jiang Jing: It's very typical of Chinese culture. You know that dragons are very important in Chinese tradition. Dragons are a positive symbol so we hope our business relations will develop positively.
Steven: That sounds good. I remember seeing a dragon dance the last time I was in China. Oh, you know we even have a dragon boat festival here every year now. They're very popular.

UNIT 6 Over to you, Exercise 2

🔊 22

Brianna: It's great to have you here today, Tuân. Just a word to our listeners about our guest – who's a faithful listener to this podcast himself, by the way. He contacted me with some interesting ideas after our last podcast on adapting behaviour to meet the expectations of business partners.

Tuân: Glad to be here, Brianna. Yes, I'd like to talk about my own experience of how and why our so-called business culture is changing.

Brianna: Please, go ahead.

Tuân: I work in the automotive industry and our teams have very international backgrounds. You can probably guess from my name that I come from a Vietnamese family, right? Well, I have colleagues from Poland, Croatia, India – all over. And others who, like me, were born in Germany, but with parents from Turkey, Kazakhstan – you name it, we probably have someone from there! But the point is, our company culture has evolved to include a variety of attitudes and behaviours. Recently a colleague from Croatia was talking about how he values punctuality, being well-organized, etc. – behaviour which seems to be "typically German" – if you can say that, but he also has kept some aspects of his "typically Croatian" ways when he invites business visitors to his home for dinner, for example. So gradually, the way we work together and with our international partners is changing anyway.

On the other hand, we shouldn't overemphasize the role of any kind of national culture. In my experience, a person's professional culture can be even more important – you know, engineers from anywhere in the world may have more in common with each other than an engineer and a marketing executive who live next door to each other.

Brianna: I'd love to hear some comments from our listeners on that. But supposing the company itself doesn't have such a multi-national staff as yours does, what happens then?

Tuân: Well, I can tell you another story about the company a friend of mine works for. The staff are not very diverse, but they do a lot of work with a variety of international partners. They can't wait for a new way of interacting with each other to evolve! At the beginning of any new projects, they sit down together – often online, of course – to discuss the ground rules of how they are going to interact with each other – so it's a bit like talking about meeting guidelines, but on a much broader scale. Topics like the importance of relationships, saying what they mean directly, preferred communication channels, for example. And the interesting thing is that the result of how they decide to move forward varies according to the specific mixture of business cultures. My friend calls this actively creating a third culture, by picking the best of both worlds. No doubt this requires a lot of flexibility from everyone and a lot of effort to start with. He says it pays off in the long run, though.

Brianna: Thanks for sharing that with us, now I'd ...

ANSWER KEY

UNIT 1

Exercise 3
A 2   B 4   C 1   D 3

Exercise 4
1 must   2 get   3 find out   4 looking forward
5 catch   6 keep   7 met   8 pronouncing

Exercise 5
a 2   b 5   c 6   d 7   e 1   f 8   g 3   h 4

Exercise 8
1 d   2 e   3 f   4 a   5 c   6 b

Exercise 9
1 sport   2 family   3 holidays   4 home
5 mutual acquaintances   6 weekend

Exercise 11
1 B   2 B   3 A

Exercise 12
1 b/g   2 d/h   3 a/c   4 e/f

Exercise 14
1 communicating   2 relationships   3 schmoozers
4 importantly   5 listening   6 interested   7 name
8 remember

Exercise 20
A 3   B 2   C 1

Exercise 21
1 time to have something   2 clearly labelled
3 a light lunch   4 have a look   5 on offer
6 a small portion   7 right here   8 food allergies
9 recommend   10 signature dish   11 you having
12 was the meal   13 who's for   14 couldn't manage

UNIT 2

Exercise 1
Correct: They're, companies, Whose, it's, yours

Exercise 2
Formal: Dear Jane Anderson / Dear Sir/Madam (This is extremely formal.)
Neutral: Good morning, Philip / Dear colleagues / Dear all / Hello, Véronique
Informal: Hi, Jessica / Hi, everyone / Stephan (Only used between people who know each other well. With others, this sounds rather unfriendly.)

Exercise 3
1 their   2 They   3 them

Exercise 4
Suggested answers:
1 Make sure your subject line matches the content of the email.
2 Focus on one topic only in an email. Keep it short and use simple language.
3 Adopt a friendly tone to start and end an email.
4 Don't write anything in an email which you don't want to be on the record.
5 Always proofread your emails to check for mistakes and appropriate tone.
6 Keep a record of phrases which are useful for the kind of emails you write.

Exercise 6
1 d   2 e   3 b   4 a   5 g   6 c   7 f   8 h

Exercise 7
1 requesting   2 thanking   3 informing
4 providing documentation   5 complaining
6 following up   7 apologizing   8 inviting

Suggested answers:
1 The writer probably wants to ask the recipient to send the price list. It sounds more like a complaint only and not a request. It may also not be clear which price list they are referring to.
"Please send me your price list for e-bike spare parts as requested in my email of 2nd March."
2 The writer probably wants to ask for an appointment with the recipient. It sounds more like a hope or a suggestion than a request.
"I would like to make an appointment to meet next week. Please suggest a date and time which is convenient for you."
3 It may not be clear which meeting the writer is referring to.
"I'm writing with regard to our meeting on Tuesday, June 12th about your new product specifications."

Exercise 10
Take care, Best, Cheers and just signing your name are informal ways of ending an email. All the others are neutral. *(Yours) sincerely* is a little more formal, but not used as often as it used to be.

Note: There is no very formal way of ending an email. In the past *Yours faithfully* and *Yours truly* were used to sign off formal letters, but this would seem extremely old-fashioned today, even in a letter.

Exercise 11
1 don't hesitate   2 hearing   3 keep me informed
4 if you need any input   5 for the weekend
6 my fingers crossed   7 day off   8 on the project
9 your thoughts   10 a good time   11 say "Hi"
12 how it went

Exercise 12
1 d   2 g   3 f   4 a   5 b   6 h   7 e   8 c

Formal: 3, 4, 5, 7, 8, d, g, h
Informal: 1, 2, 6, a, b, c, e, f

Exercise 13
Suggested answers regarding the style of emails 1-4:
1 Formal, neutral with standard phrases only.
2 Businesslike, not focussing on politeness but in a way that suggests they know each other well so is not unfriendly. This may be one of a chain of emails back and forth. It is also an urgent matter.
3 Informal, friendly and suggests they know each other well. He hints that Elena is putting him under a bit of pressure.
4 Businesslike and relatively formal. She is writing to the whole team so may have different relationships with individual members. It is a standard thank-you email at the end of a project.

Exercise 14
Email 2: The request for action is very direct and must be complied with urgently. Sounds almost like an order.
"Please send your list of questions to Mike and Pavel without delay."
Email 3: The request for action is more diplomatic and gives the impression that it's up to the recipient to comply or not.
"Anyway, I'm writing to ask if you could send me an update on the status of the construction work."

Note: Although the tone is different, the writer in each case expects to get the requested information asap.

Exercise 17
1 T   2 F   3 T   4 T   5 F   6 T

Exercise 18
Benefits: saves time, a good way to learn suitable words and phrases and spot mistakes, gives confidence
Drawbacks: depends on the quality of the prompts, less useful for very specialized content, still a need to check that the tone and content is what you want, uncertainty about the legal situation

OVER TO YOU, Exercise 2
1 When we meet in June, we can discuss our options.
2 To get a grant, we need to apply in writing by January 30th.
3 So far this year, the company has saved €150,000 on storage costs.
4 The project team aims to standardize our payroll system.
5 May I ask you to let me know what you recommend?
6 Please confirm the date and time of our meeting next week.
7 We expect profits to remain stable for the next quarter.
8 We intend to increase our production capacity in the future.

ANSWER KEY

UNIT 3

Exercise 3
Some possible differences you may notice when comparing an English and a German written text are:
- German more often uses nouns where English tends to use verbs
- German sentences tend to be longer and may be more precisely formulated
- German uses a more impersonal, neutral tone including more use of passive voice whereas English uses personal pronouns and active voice
- English texts tend to be shorter than German texts with the same content

Exercise 5
1 c 2 e 3 d 4 a 5 b

Exercise 7
Message 1:
- caller: Tomas
- reason for call: list of special offers for premium customers
- action required: email the figures by tomorrow morning

Message 2:
- caller: Julia Chen
- reason for call: asking for hotel booking confirmation
- action required: send the confirmation asap

Message 3:
- caller: Martin
- reason for call: confirming a meeting appointment and offering to discuss the agenda
- action required: send the agenda if possible

Exercise 9
B: 3, 5, 6, 8, 9, 11
E: 1, 2, 4, 7, 10, 12

caller: 1, 3, 4, 6, 8
recipient: 5, 7, 9
both: 2, 10, 11, 12

Exercise 11
1 c 2 e 3 f 4 a 5 b 6 d

2e, 3f and 6d could be used at the beginning of a telephone call which has been pre-planned by the caller and the recipient.

Exercise 12
1 have time for 2 until early evening
3 How about 4 suit you 5 particular time
6 any time after that 7 Shall we say 8 work for
9 Let me just check

Exercise 14
1 b 2 a 3 a 4 b

Exercise 17
1 B 2 A 3 B 4 A 5 B 6 A 7 A 8 B 9 B
10 A 11 B 12 A

Exercise 23
1 c 2 d 3 b 4 e 5 a

Exercise 24
- get hold of + reach
- breaking up + the phone signal is poor
- return a call + call back
- keep in contact + stay in touch
- ring off + end the conversation
- lose contact + cut off
- give someone a buzz + call someone

Exercise 26
Step 1: d, l, f
Step 2: b, e, h
Step 3: a, g, c

Exercise 27
1 speaking 2 short notice 3 How's the weather
4 take up too much 5 breaking up 6 is very poor
7 didn't catch 8 make a suggestion
9 check my schedule 10 work

UNIT 4

Warm-up
1 hybrid working, back-to-the-office
2 workspace design, barrier-free access
3 four-day-week
4 flexible working hours, teamwork skills
5 forced fun
6 diverse workforce, corporate language policies
7 carbon footprint, paper-light office

Exercise 5
a silent pod   b soft-seating area   c hot-desking bench   d quiet zone   e meeting booth
f informal meeting area

Exercise 6
Antonia shows Dominic: c, b, a, d

1 let me show you around
2 a look around
3 for our present needs
4 reduced our capacity
5 look over there
6 on each floor
7 over there in the corner
8 for making telephone calls or working
9 if people need to
10 walk over to

a 1, 2, 5, 6, 7, 10
b 3, 4, 8, 9

Exercise 8
e, f, a, b, c, d

Exercise 9
1 c   2 e   3 a   4 d   5 f   6 b

Exercise 14
Active verbs: took, showed, gave
Passive verbs: were shown, were taken, were offered

Exercise 16
1 g   2 e   3 h   4 b   5 a   6 c   7 f   8 d

Opinions may vary about the most logical order. Suggested answer:
5/a   2/e   7/f   3/h   1/g   4/b   6/c   8/d

Exercise 17
1 Please keep together at all times.
2 Before we go in, please put on the protective clothing.
3 Just over on the left, you can see the entrance to out R&D lab.
4 If everyone has had a chance to see everything, shall we head over to …
5 This is where we manufacture parts for trucks.
6 You mentioned that this line has the most downtime, right?
7 Let's make our way back to the conference room. I'm sure that some refreshments are waiting for us.

Exercise 18
1 lose   2 free   3 state-of-the-art   4 replacing
5 does it take   6 walk over

Exercise 19
1 b, f   2 d, h   3 a, g   4 c, e

ANSWER KEY

UNIT 5

Exercise 3
1 started, come   2 turn (switch is also possible)
3 role   4 better, move

1 c   2 a   3 d   4 b

an online meeting: 2   a kick-off meeting: 3
a debriefing: 4   a brainstorming meeting: 1

Exercise 7
If you prefer, use this template for effective ground rules as a basis for your English version.

Lege eine Agenda mit einem klaren Ziel für das Meetings fest. Beachte das Zeitmodell mit eingeplantem Puffer:
- *30 Min: 5 Min Puffer*
- *60-90 Min: 10 Min Puffer*

Sorge für eine klare Rollenverteilung:
- *Moderator*in*
- *Expert*in*
- *Protokollant*in*
- *Technische(r) Moderator*in*

Sorge für die Bereitstellung aller nötigen Tools. Halte die Teilnehmer*innenzahl möglichst gering. Vermeide Überziehung des zeitlichen Rahmens. Bleibe bei dem vorgegebenen Diskussionsrahmen (zielgerichtet).

Achte auf Umgangsformen:
- *Begrüßung am Anfang*
- *Mikrofon nur bei Bedarf einschalten*
- *Wortmeldung bei Unterbrechung*
- *Bleibe immer aufmerksam*

Exercise 10
1 b   2 d   3 a   4 c

Suggested answers:
1
- Let's turn our attention to the next point on the agenda.
- If no one has anything else to add, I suggest we move on to the next item.

2
- Please just give me a few seconds to finish what I was saying.
- Afra is making an important point so please let her finish.

3
- We have to close the meeting very soon, so please keep the discussion focused.
- I suggest saving that issue for our next meeting.

4
- I'd appreciate everyone's input on this topic.
- Let's hear your thoughts on this, Stefan.

Exercise 11
1 make   2 position   3 hear   4 concerns
5 mind   6 with

Tell us what you are worried about: 4, 5
Did I make myself clear: 1, 6
Tell us your opinion: 2, 3

Exercise 12
- attend, take part in
- chair, facilitate, host, moderate
- circulate, send round
- compile, draw up
- hold, run
- join, log in to
- solve, sort out

Exercise 13
1 g, k   2 h, l   3 a, i   4 b, f   5 d, j   6 c, e

Exercise 15
1 Jessica is sticking to the guidelines that meetings always start on time.
2 Rohan says that the spreadsheets with sales figures are ready to be distributed to the team.
3
- takeaways: the key points which emerge from a discussion or, in this case, sales results
- bringing someone up to speed: give someone the latest information on a specific topic
- problems down the line: problems that may occur in the future

4 Rohan is having difficulty reaching the software developers.
5 Marta didn't have the same problem as Rohan. She was able to contact the software developer.
6 Jessica interrupts Marta because she wants her to explain the situation at the software developers to Rohan in a one-to-one conversation. It's not a topic for the present meeting.

Exercise 16
1 e   2 d   3 a   4 f   5 b   6 c

Exercise 18
1 d   2 c   3 a   4 b

Exercise 19
1 support   2 platforms   3 individual   4 function
5 breakout   6 monitor   7 sessions   8 thread

Exercise 23
1 Rosa has joined the meeting from Porto.
2 The Portuguese supplier covers the whole range of shoes they sell (from high-end leather to sports shoes) so they wouldn't need to deal with two different suppliers (in China and Italy).
3 The background image shows the city of Porto.
4 Liam offers to monitor the chat for any comments or questions while Rosa is speaking.
5 Rosa is going to talk about sustainability issues, the products, the manufacturing plant.
6 They mention recycling rates, carbon footprint, supply chain sustainability.

Exercise 25
1 understand   2 saying   3 misunderstood   4 put   5 follow   6 meant   7 getting

Exercise 26
1 d   2 e   3 a   4 c   5 b   6 f

OVER TO YOU, Exercise 2
1 e   2 a   3 f   4 g   5 b   6 d   7 c   8 h

UNIT 6

Exercise 6
2 The English translations are very similar, but not 100% the same.
- We're all in the same boat.
- You have to read between the lines.

Note: The post-it refers to 57 European languages. There are 50 countries which are wholly or partly in Europe. 24 languages are recognized as official EU languages, but in fact Europe is home to as many as 200 languages. These include languages such as Basque, Catalan and Sami.

4 In general, if you want to use an idiomatic phrase in a lingua franca context, it's a good idea to additionally offer an explanation in English. Even if there are English language equivalents, they may not mean what you intend, and your conversation partners may not understand them either.

The original German idioms are:
- "Vorsicht ist die Mutter der Porzellankiste."
An English idiomatic phrase which carries a similar message is "Better safe than sorry."
- "Der Knoten ist geplatzt."
"Everything clicked into place" is close to some uses of the German phrase but will not always have the meaning you intend.

Exercise 7
Suggested answers:
- I'm sure we're all on the same page here. = I'm sure we all agree on this.
- Let's circle back on this at the next meeting. = Let's return to this topic at the next meeting.
- You should focus on your core competency, and that is market analysis. = You should focus on your main strength, and that is market analysis.
- I think it's time for a deep dive. = I think it's time for a thorough analysis of the situation.
- Moving our production to Bulgaria is going to be a game changer. = Moving our production to Bulgaria is going to have a significant impact.
- Dealing with so many logistical challenges is like herding cats. = Dealing with so many logistical challenges is almost impossible to do.
- We should leverage the expertise of our sales team. = We should make the most of the expertise of our sales team.
- Making these changes to our workflow was a no-brainer in my opinion. = Making these changes to our workflow was a very easy decision to make.
- We need to think outside the box if we want to solve this problem. = We need to explore some creative and unusual ways of solving this problem.
- How can we utilize the skills of our team? = How can we use the talents of our team?

Note: You may hear a lot of business jargon in your job, but not everyone will understand the phrases. The best way to communicate yourself is to say what you mean in clear and simple language. In addition, many idiomatic phrases become clichés and may sound old-fashioned.

Exercise 8
1 go through   **2** put off   **3** turn down
4 have called off   **5** went on   **6** find out
7 get back   **8** had drawn up

Exercise 9
In Kenya, a merry-go-round can refer to an informal cooperative savings scheme typically run by women.

Exercise 15
Note: In all situations in the exercise, what people consider to be a polite reaction depends on personal preferences which may, or not, be influenced by behaviour norms within the company and general cultural norms. The relationship between the people concerned will often also play a role.

Suggested answers:
1 Reactions can vary between making no comment at all to avoid drawing attention to the fact the person isn't looking well and commenting in order to show concern.
"Are you feeling OK?" | "You're looking a bit tired. Can I get you a coffee?"
2 If one of the meeting ground rules is having your phone switched off, it would be appropriate to say sorry and switch it off. However, if you are expecting a very important call, it might be necessary to apologize and say that you have to take the call and leave the meeting room.
"I'm sorry but I have to take this call. It's a very urgent matter. I'll be back in a moment."
3 You may just let it go and not comment at all. If you want to mention it, you can say something like "Actually, my name is … It's quite difficult to pronounce, I know!"
4 You may just say thank you and give the person your card. In some cultures, exchanging business cards is an important ritual. In that case, it is a good idea to look carefully at the card and make a comment about the company or the person's role as mentioned in exercise 11.

5 Reactions may vary between being quite open about not understanding and asking your manager to explain again and just nodding as if you understand. There may be personal or cultural reasons for thinking that you lose face if you don't understand what you have to do.

6 People who prefer direct communication will likely just say that they have no time to meet and possibly suggest another more suitable time.

"I'm sorry, but I'm just too busy at the moment. How about meeting at the end of next week? Would that suit you?"

In some cultural contexts, saying no directly seems impolite so they may say something like "I'll try to meet you then, but it may be difficult." In fact, this means that they have no time to meet.

Exercise 16
Suggested answers:
1
- Would you have a moment to come to my office after your lunch break? There's something I'd like to talk to you about.
- I was wondering if you could come to my office after your lunch break.

2
- Our sales figures for last year were not as good as we had expected.
- I'm afraid that our sales figures for last year were rather disappointing.

3
- Don't you think we should replace our lab equipment? It doesn't seem quite fit for purpose anymore.
- I'm afraid we'll have to replace most of the equipment in our lab as it no longer meets our needs.

4
- I wonder if you could be more specific.
- I'm afraid that I need more specific details.

5
- Don't you think we should check the figures again?
- I think it would be quite a good idea to recheck the figures.

6
- Can I ask you to send me the report by Friday, please?
- Would you send me the report by Friday? It's rather urgent!

7
- Unfortunately, the project team didn't do a very good job.
- The project team's work was rather disappointing to be honest.

8
- I was wondering if you could arrange an earlier delivery.
- I'm sorry but we need to receive the delivery earlier than that.

Exercise 17
In each case, the speaker may mean exactly what they say. However, people who prefer an indirect communication style may in fact mean the following:

1 I'm pretty certain that it's not my fault.
2 This is what I really wanted to talk to you about.
3 It's not going to work so don't go ahead as planned.
4 That's a very strange opinion.
5 We have a major problem.

Exercise 21
Polite: 3, 4, 5
Impolite: 1, 2, 6

Exercise 23
1 f   2 g   3 h   4 b   5 c   6 d   7 i   8 j   9 e   10 a

USEFUL PHRASES

The phrases below will be useful tools in your work. Highlight phrases which are particularly relevant to you and look at them regularly to help you remember them.

Additionally, you will find interactive exercises in the **Cornelsen Lernen App** expanding on the Useful Phrases provided in this book.

GETTING STARTED

EXCHANGING CONTACT DETAILS

Offering printed cards
1. May I give you my card?
2. Shall we exchange contact details? Here's my card.
3. Here are my contact details if you have a query.
4. By the way, here's my card. Don't hesitate to contact me.

Responding
- Thank you. Here's mine.
- Great, thanks. Oh no, I've run out of cards. Can I give you my email address instead?
- Thanks. Let me give you my card.
- Thanks. I'll be in touch

Offering virtual contact details
1. I'll send you a connection request now via social media. I'm sure you use this app? What's your full name?
2. Would you like to share your contact details?
3. I'll send you my digital card by email.

- Yes, I do. My name is Chris Price.

- Sure. Just scan my digital card. Here's the QR code.
- I have a card in my email signature, too.

SHIFTING THE FOCUS OF A CONVERSATION

- OK then everyone, shall we make a start?
- Right, if everyone's finished their coffee, let's get started.
- It's 11.30 already, so shall we start the meeting?
- Well, we have a lot on the agenda for today so I think it's time to start.
- We have a new team member so let's start with a round of introductions.
- Anyway, there's something I'd like to ask you about the project schedule.
- Well, I suppose now would be a good time to look at latest sales figures.

TRANSITIONING FROM SMALL TALK TO BUSINESS ON THE PHONE

- Well, the project is going well, thanks. We're very busy just now so what was it you wanted to speak to me about?
- Listen, (*name of caller*), I'm sorry but I have an online meeting in a few minutes so tell me why …
- Well, that's nice to hear (*after some positive news from the caller*). So, how can I help you?
- I'm glad you've called because I've been meaning to contact you myself. Are you calling about …?
- Anyway, I suppose you're calling about …

EMAIL WRITING

OPENING AND CLOSING PHRASES

Starting an email
- I hope this finds you well.
- I know how busy you are, so I'll be brief.
- Thanks for getting back to me so quickly with the sales figures.
- How have you been since we last spoke?
- I was so pleased that we were able to meet up again last week.

Stating the reason for writing
- As requested, please find attached the …
- We are very sorry for the inconvenience caused by …
- Thank you very much for …
- I really appreciate your help in …
- I'd like to welcome you to …

Ending an email
- I look forward to hearing from you.
- If you have any further questions, don't hesitate to contact me.
- Just give me a call if you need any input from our side.
- Don't forget to say "Hi" to Renzo from me.
- Looking forward to working with you on the project.

- I'm pleased to announce that …
- I must apologize for …
- I'm writing to remind you to …
- I'm afraid that we are not …
- Could you …

SETTING THE RIGHT TONE

Writing informally
- Sorry I haven't got back to you sooner.
- Great to hear from you.
- Thanks for your heads up about the meeting.

Expressing urgency
- This is a very urgent matter.
- Please … without further delay.
- We must solve this by tomorrow / asap.
- Please make this a priority.

Being diplomatic
- I'd like to ask you a favour. Could you …?
- I know you are busy, but …
- I look forward to receiving …

Showing gratitude
- I would be grateful if you could help me out.
- Thanks in advance!
- This would be very helpful.

ON THE PHONE

PROBLEMS WITH PHONE CALLS

Technical problems
- It's a very bad line.
- My battery's low.
- Does your battery need charging?
- Hello? You're breaking up.
- I couldn't get a signal.
- We were cut off.

Ending a phone call
- Well, I have a meeting very shortly so …
- It's been great talking to you.
- I'll look forward to your email.

Problems understanding
- I'm sorry, I didn't catch that.
- Could you speak up a bit, please?
- Would you mind slowing down a bit?
- Could you repeat the name of …?
- Could you explain that in a different way?
- I'm sorry, but I can't follow you.

- So, don't let me take up any more of your time.
- We'll talk again soon. Take care.
- Thanks again and until next time.

USEFUL PHRASES

COMMUNICATING AT WORK

EXPRESSING OPINIONS

Giving your opinion
- As far as I know, …
- It seems to me that …
- It's important to note that …
- Well, if you ask me, I think …
- I can't imagine how …
- One thing that I've noticed is …

Expressing doubt / disagreement
- You have a point, but …
- Yes, but don't you think that …
- I see what you mean, but …
- I'm sorry, but I don't agree with you on that.

Checking understanding
- Sorry, my English is not so good. Did you say?
- Did you say first or third?
- So, you're saying …
- So, to confirm …
- Can I just check that I understood that right?
- Believe it or not, I've never spoken to anyone from … before.

Summarizing people's opinions
- Generally speaking, all of them think …
- On the whole, …
- … seem(s) to think that …
- They appear to agree that …
- One drawback seems to be …
- The main benefits they mention are …

Showing agreement
- Absolutely.
- Exactly.
- That's true.
- That's just what I was thinking.

- Have I got this right? You said …
- So, do you mean …?
- Let me see if I got that right.
- If I've understood you correctly, …
- What was that word again?

FACILITATING A MEETING

Telling people what is expected tactfully and professionally
- I'd like to start by reminding everyone of our meeting guidelines.
- Let's aim to finish the meeting on time by avoiding distractions.
- Please don't forget to click on the raise hand button if you want to contribute.
- We appreciate your input, Jaime. Thanks. Now, let's hear from the others. Tom?
- Assuming that everyone has read the agenda, let's start with our first item.
- Let's come back to this next time when Gillian can explain what she meant.
- I don't think I need to tell you how important it is to stay on topic.
- As you can see, our client has given us a very tight schedule.

Encouraging participation
- Let's have a quick update from everyone on what they've been doing.
- Our goal today is to identify the obstacles to delivering the project on time.
- Can I ask everyone to share their concerns about the project?
- I'd like to hear from each of you on this.

Talking about potential risks
- It's highly likely that …
- It's possible that …
- We have to take into account that …
- There's a great risk of …

- It's pretty unlikely that … unless …
- There's a slight chance that …
- There some hope that …
- There's very little hope of …

PRESENTING

Giving an overview of the presentation topics
- I'd like to cover a number of topics related to …
- I'd like to give you a breakdown of the opportunities …

Describing the structure of a presentation
- I'll start with …
- I'd like to walk you through …
- Then I'll move on to …
- Then finally, I'll talk about …

Describing content
- OK, so let me outline …
- I think it's important to highlight the fact that …

Presenting in an online meeting
- Let me know if the sound quality isn't good enough.
- I want to share my screen with you.
- Let me share the document so that you can …
- I'll adjust the zoom settings to make it easier to read.
- Roman will be monitoring the chat for any comments or questions you have.

Transitioning
- OK, let's move on to the next point.
- This brings me to …
- Right, now for …

Ending a presentation
- Let me finish by answering any questions you may have.
- That brings me to the end of …

COMPANY TOURS

Guiding visitors
- Please follow me down the stairs to the production area.
- Please keep together at all times.
- Before we go in, please put on this protective clothing.
- So now, let's go into the lab.
- Do you have any questions before we move on?
- If everyone has had the chance to see everything here, shall we head over to the shop floor?

Questions to ask
- You mentioned earlier that this line has the most downtime, right?
- Are you planning to phase out the equipment?
- How long does it take to retool the line when you switch to the new technology?

Pointing things out
- So, this is where we manufacture parts for trucks.
- Just over on the left, you can see the entrance to our R&D lab.
- I'd like to draw your attention to our new production line for electric vehicles. It's really state-of-the-art.
- Behind that door is the control room.
- The quality control department is beyond the second production hall.
- Coming up now is something which I know will interest you all.

Finishing the tour
- Well, that brings us to the end of the tour for today.
- I hope I've been able to give you some insight into our manufacturing processes.
- Let's make our way back to the conference room. I'm sure that some refreshments are waiting for us!

A-Z WORDLIST

A
accuracy   sprachliche Richtigkeit
to acquire sth   etw. erwerben, erlangen
agenda item   Tagesordnungspunkt
to aim to do sth   etw. anstreben
to allocate roles   Rollen verteilen
to allow for sth   *hier:* etw. einplanen
to anticipate sth   etw. voraussehen
appropriate   angemessen
artificial intelligence (AI)   künstliche Intelligenz (KI)
as a matter of course   wie selbstverständlich
at short notice   kurzfristig

B
banned   untersagt
barrier-free access   Barrierefreiheit
behaviours   Verhaltensweisen, Auftreten
to boost sth   etw. verstärken, verbessern
to bore so   jmdn. langweilen
the bottom line   Nettoergebnis, Endresultat
branch office   Zweigstelle
a bribe / bribery   Bestechung
businesslike   sachlich

C
carbon footprint CO_2-Fußabdruck
to carry out sth   etw. durchführen
casual   zwanglos
challenging   schwierig, herausfordernd
a choice of   eine Auswahl an
clear-cut   eindeutig
collaborative work   gemeinschaftliches Arbeiten
to come into force   in Kraft treten
to commute   pendeln
company-issued   firmeneigen
confident   zuversichtlich
confidential   vertraulich
considerate   rücksichtsvoll
consumption   Verbrauch

to contribute to sth   *hier:* zur Diskussion beitragen | *hier:* sich in etw. einbringen
controversial   strittig, brisant
credibility   Glaubwürdigkeit
cross-functional   funktionsübergreifend
crucial   von entscheidender Bedeutung

D
delivery   *hier:* Vortragsweise
to determine sth   etw. festlegen
to dial   wählen
dietary needs   Ernährungsanforderungen
digitized   digitalisiert
distraction   Ablenkung
to do what it takes   tun was nötig ist

E
to ensure sth   *hier:* für etw. sorgen
to estimate   schätzen
to evolve   sich entwickeln
expanding   wachsend
expansion   Erweiterung
extension   Durchwahl

F
to familiarize so with sth   jmdn. mit etw. vertraut machen
far-reaching   weitreichend
to feel connected to sth   sich etw. verbunden fühlen
to figure sth out   etw. herausfinden
forced fun   erzwungener Spaß
frequency   Häufigkeit

G
to get a word in   zu Wort kommen
get-together   Beisammensein, Treffen
goal-oriented   zielgerichtet
to go back to normal   zur Normalität zurückkehren
to go the extra mile   sich ins Zeug legen

H
to have a say in sth   bei etw. Mitspracherecht haben
to head back   zurückfahren, zurückgehen
to hear so out   jmdn. ausreden lassen
to hold the line   am Apparat bleiben

I
to implement sth   etw. umsetzen
ingredient   Zutat
intelligibility   Verständlichkeit
in the long run   auf lange Sicht
to involve sth   etw. beinhalten

K
key point   Eckpunkt

L
landline   Festnetz
lavish   verschwenderisch, üppig
leeway   Zeitpuffer
to lose sight of sth/so   *hier:* etw./jmdn. vernachlässigen

M
machine translation   maschinelle Übersetzung
to make sth available   etw. bereitstellen
minutes (of a meeting)   Protokoll
mistaken   irrtümlich
to mute a mic   Mikrofon stummschalten
mutual acquaintances   gemeinsame Bekannte

N
new hires   neu eingestellte Mitarbeiter*innen
notably   in besonderem Maße
to not have a clue   keinen Schimmer haben

O
on the road   *hier:* unterwegs
on top of that   obendrein
to overrun (time)   überziehen
to oversee sth/so   etw./jmdn. betreuen
overwhelmed   *hier:* überlastet

P

personal communication direkter Austausch
plant *hier:* Fabrik, Werk
(business) premises (pl.) Geschäftsräume, Betriebsgebäude
to **pre-plan sth** etw. vorplanen
to **promote sth** *hier:* etw. fördern
to **proofread sth** etw. Korrektur lesen
to **put so through** jmdn. durchstellen

R

to **reassign sth** *hier:* etw. neu zuweisen
recipient Empfänger*in
to **redesign sth** etw. umgestalten
to **redirect sth** *hier:* etw. verbinden
relieved erleichtert
reluctant widerwillig, zurückhaltend
to **rely on sth** sich auf etw. verlassen
to **reprioritize sth** für etw. neue Prioritäten setzen
reserved zurückhaltend
to **revisit sth** etw. überdenken

S

to **secure sth** *hier:* etw. gewinnen
to **set so back** jmdn. viel Geld kosten
shop floor Fertigung
to **shrink** schrumpfen
signal strength Signalstärke
signature dish Spezialität des Hauses
smart *hier:* intelligent
snap survey Kurzumfrage
some give and take ein gegenseitiges Geben und Nehmen
spicy food scharfes Essen
to **splash out on sth** für etw. tief in die Tasche greifen
to **spot sth** etw. entdecken
spread Verbreitung
to **stick to sth** bei etw. bleiben
straightforward einfach, unkompliziert
subject matter Materie, Thematik
subsidiary Niederlassung, Tochterunternehmen
suitable geeignet
sustainable nachhaltig
a switch to sth ein Wechsel zu etw.
to **switch to sth** zu etw. wechseln
switchboard, main line Zentrale

T

to **tailor sth to so** etw. auf jmdn. zuschneiden
to **take sth into account** etw. berücksichtigen
to **take part in sth** an etw. teilnehmen
to **take place** stattfinden
to **take so away from sth** jmdn. von etw. abhalten
to **take up (time)** (Zeit) in Anspruch nehmen
the nuts and bolts die praktischen Grundlagen
tight schedule straffer Zeitplan
to **tighten sth up** etw. verschärfen, festigen
a token of sth *hier:* ein Zeichen von etw.
to **transfer a call** einen Anruf weiterleiten
tricky schwierig
typo Tippfehler

U

urgency Dringlichkeit

V

to **value sth/so** etw./jmdn. wertschätzen
values (pl.) Werte
vegetarian vegetarisch, Vegetarier*in

KEY VERBS FOR YOUR JOB

to access	Our customers are complaining about having trouble **accessing** the data.	auf etw. zugreifen
to **achieve**	I'm pleased to report that the sales team has **achieved** remarkable results.	erreichen
to **affect**	We hope that the new government regulations are not going to **affect** small businesses like ours.	betreffen, sich auswirken
to **appreciate**	While we greatly **appreciate** your input, I wonder if you could be more specific about the actual cost of what you're suggesting.	schätzen
to **assign**	Before we finish today, I'd like to **assign** some tasks for the next meeting.	zuweisen
to **confirm**	I'm still waiting for the supplier in Mexico to **confirm** the delivery.	bestätigen
to **consider**	As far as I know, management has agreed to **consider** allowing staff to continue working from home on at least two days per week.	in Betracht ziehen
to **contribute**	It's obvious that the meeting went very well because everyone **contributed** to the discussion in a very constructive way.	beitragen
to **ensure**	Thanks to everyone in the project team we have **ensured** that we have delivered a top quality product on time.	gewährleisten
to **estimate**	The aim of the study was to **estimate** the effects of our e-mobility policy on our present customer base.	abschätzen
to **face**	As environmental regulations become stricter, we're **facing** the challenge of keeping transport costs down.	mit etw. konfrontiert sein
to **fulfil**	I'm glad to say that many of our applicants **fulfil** the requirements.	erfüllen
to **implement**	Since we **implemented** our inclusion strategy, we've noticed a definite increase in staff motivation levels.	umsetzen
to **invoice**	Our policy is that we **invoice** only after the work has been completed and accepted by the customer.	in Rechnung stellen
to **maintain**	As we always aim to **maintain** the highest quality standards in our products, I was very sorry to hear that you are not satisfied.	aufrechterhalten
to **manufacture**	Some of the components for our latest model are **manufactured** in Romania and then assembled at the plant in Germany.	herstellen
to **monitor**	I've been **monitoring** the market very closely for a few months now and would like to update you on my findings.	überwachen, beobachten
to **postpone**	We've had to **postpone** the product launch by two months.	verschieben
to **process**	We only share your personal data with third parties when this is necessary to **process** an order.	bearbeiten, abwickeln
to **reject**	We're looking for a new supplier in China because our inspectors have had to **reject** too many pieces from our current partner.	etw. zurückweisen
to **rely on**	We're **relying on** our R&D department to come up with innovative products which will sell well on the Asian market.	auf etw. verlassen
to **revisit**	There have been so many problems marketing the latest model that we have no choice but to **revisit** our complete sales strategy.	etw. wiederaufgreifen
to **schedule**	Management is going to announce some far-reaching changes in company policy so they have **scheduled** an all-hands for Tuesday.	terminieren, ansetzen
to **ship**	In order to reduce costs, we're asking the supplier to **ship** the merchandise in one batch.	verschicken, versenden
to **submit**	If we want to **submit** a proposal to the shareholders' meeting, I'd like to remind you that the deadline is in one week.	einreichen, vorlegen